C0-DUR-503

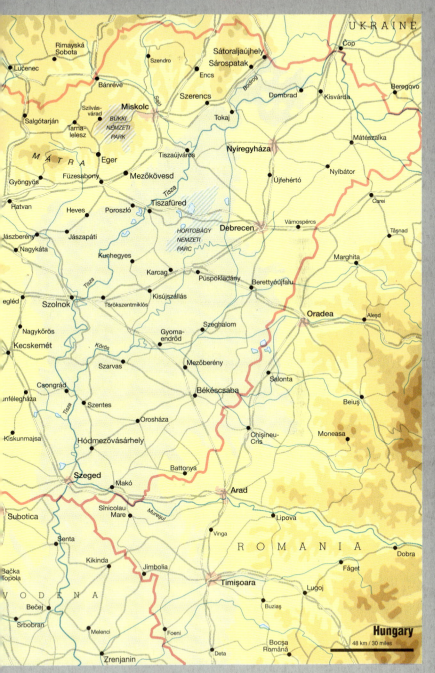

UKRAINE

Rimayská
Sobota
Lučenec
Bánréve
Szendro
Sátoraljaújhely
Sárospatak
Čop
Szilvás-
várad
Miskolc
Encs
Szerencs
Dombrad
Beregovó
Salgótarján
Tarna-
lelesz
BÜKKI
NEMZETI
PARK
Sajo
Tokaj
Kisvárda
Mátészalka
MÁTRA
Eger
Tiszaújváros
Nyíregyháza
Gyöngyös
Füzesabony
Mezőkövesd
Tisza
Nyílbátor
Hatvan
Heves
Poroszló
Tiszafüred
Újfehértó
Carei
Jászberény
Jászapáti
HORTOBÁGY
NEMZETI
PARC
Debrecen
Vámospércs
Tăşnad
Nagykáta
Kunhegyes
Karcag
Püspökladány
Berettyóújfalu
Marghita
Tisza
Kisújszállás
egléd
Szolnok
Törökszentmiklós
Oradea
Aleşd
Nagykőrös
Kecskemét
Körös
Gyoma-
endrőd
Szarvas
Szeghalom
Salonta
Beiuş
Csongrád
Mezőberény
unfélegyháza
Szentes
Tisza
Békéscsaba
Moneasa
Orosháza
Kiskunmajsa
Hódmezővásárhely
Chişineu-
Criş
Szeged
Makó
Battonya
Arad
Subotica
Sînicolau
Mare
Mureşul
Lipová
Senta
Vinga
ROMANIA
Bačka
Topola
Kikinda
Jimbolia
Dobra
Făget
VODENA
Timişoara
Lugoj
Bečej
Buziaş
Srbobran
Melenci
Foeni
Bocşa
Română
Hungary
Deta
48 km / 30 miles
Zrenjanin

Hungary and Europe

750 km / 470 miles

INSIGHT *POCKET* GUIDES

HUNGARY

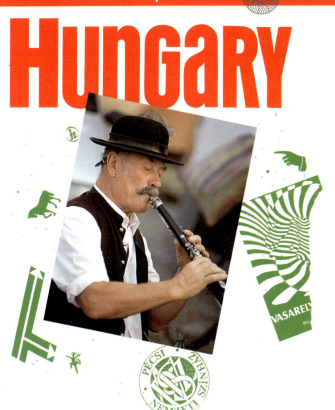

Written and Presented by **Márton Radkai**

INSIGHT
pocket
GUIDES

Insight Pocket Guide:

HUNGARY

Directed by
Hans Höfer

Managing Editor
Tony Halliday

Photography by
Márton Radkai

Design Concept by
V. Barl

Design by
Carlotta Junger

© 1994 APA Publications (HK) Ltd

All Rights Reserved

Printed in Singapore by
Höfer Press (Pte) Ltd
Fax: 65-8616438

Distributed in the United States by
Houghton Mifflin Company
222 Berkeley Street
Boston, Massachusetts 02116-3764
ISBN: 0-395-69965-7

Distributed in Canada by
Thomas Allen & Son
390 Steelcase Road East
Markham, Ontario L3R 1G2
ISBN: 0-395-69965-7

Distributed in the UK & Ireland by
GeoCenter International UK Ltd
The Viables Center, Harrow Way
Basingstoke, Hampshire RG22 4BJ
ISBN: 9-62421-583-9

Worldwide distribution enquiries:
Höfer Communications Pte Ltd
38 Joo Koon Road
Singapore 2262
ISBN: 9-62421-583-9

JÓ napot!

Márton Radkai

I first travelled to Hungary in 1988, a trip that paved the way to my work editing the *Insight Guide: Hungary*, but my intimate involvement with the country was launched decades before, when my parents decided to name me Márton after my grandfather. This Hungarian form of Martin maintained an ephemeral link to an unknown land. Moreover, my grandfather had been a famous actor, comedian and singer until his death in 1951, and for as long as I can remember, his compatriots, from shopkeepers to anaesthetists, have heaped praise on his talents with damp eyes. My curiosity was needled.

Hungary always lurked on the periphery, my father cooking, counting and cursing in Hungarian, struggling with the fingering and unusual rhythms of Bartók and longing to play Liszt rhapsodies on the piano, devouring Molnár's *The Paul Street Boys* on Sundays. In school I admired the diplomatic feats of Deák and Andrássy, the heroic struggles against the Habsburgs and the tragedy of 1956. I noted Hungarian feats, from the destructive physics of Edward Teller to the constructive physique of Ilona Staller, from the helicopter and the match, to the Biro (ballpoint pen in US English), Rubik's cube, Arpád Elo's chess ratings, and the brilliant logic of using Mig reactors to blow out oil-fires in Kuwait in 1991.

The Hungarians and their land are odd bedfellows, and the incongruity a reminder of the nomadic origins of the Magyars. The people are extrovert, fickle, brazen, talkative, whereas the landscape is melancholy and subtle.

Hungary boasts no spectacular sights. It consists of a host of details, splinters of beauty, hundreds of vignettes. Twenty-five trips on, after around 65,000 km (40,000 miles) on Hungarian roads, I am still collecting impressions, some of which I would like to share with you in the following pages. *Jó napot – Welcome!*

Contents

Preceding pages:
the hot-water lake at Hévíz

Following pages: men of the
Puszta – the Hungarian plain

HISTORY &

The history of Hungary is the history of a stretch of land extending from the Carpathians to the foothills of the Alps, settled and visited by a host of tribes and peoples – Celts, Slavs, Avars, Sarmatians, Romans, Huns, Goths and Vandals – whose remains can be seen in museums throughout the country. The history of Hungary, however, is also the history of the Magyar people who, though they themselves would like to see it otherwise, were nothing but a scourge to western Europe at one time. Their warriors, riding small, fast horses, descended on settlements as far west as Alsace, killing, raping and looting. They reminded their victims of a previous band of misfits known as the Onogurs (hence the misnomer Hungarian) but they were of a different origin: they came from somewhere east of the Urals, and over a period of about 4,000 years moved west.

Kálmán I

The Magyars arrived in the Carpathian Basin in 896, led by Árpád, and served as mercenaries to whomever paid best, picking up odds and ends along the way. This period, euphemistically referred to by the Hungarians as the 'Time of Adventure' (*kalandozás*), ended when they ran up against the heavily armed knights of Otto I in 955 near Augsburg. The Magyars got the message and settled down. Prince Géza, a descendant of Árpád, began negotiating with western and Byzantine leaders. He remained a heathen, not wishing to irritate his subjects, but had his son István baptised and primed for the kingdom. The Pope gave his blessings to the new state in 1001.

Culture

12th-century coin

The Árpáds

István I, who was later canonised, created the infrastructure for a modern state and a set of laws combining Christian and heathen elements. There were ten bishoprics (including Esztergom, his seat, Eger, Kalocsa and Székesfehérvár), a number of centres with forts (*vár* in Hungarian means fortress and is a common suffix in town names) for the *ispáns*, the king's delegates who would later become known as barons or magnates, with their own independent military forces.

When István died in 1038, all was not as well with the country as he had hoped. His only son Imre (Emmerich) had died in 1031 and the question of succession brought a number of impoverished kings and usurpers to the throne; this alternation between a strong king, able to keep the internal, rival factions at bay, and total chaos was to become a recurring pattern in Hungarian history. László I (1077–95), also later canonised, put Hungary in order, ruling with an iron hand. He moved into Croatia too and down to the Dalmatian coast on the Adriatic. He was succeeded by Kálmán I, a remarkably enlightened and shrewd ruler, whose love of books earned him the nickname *könyves*, 'bookish'.

Béla III (1172–96) was another great Hungarian king. Born and raised in Constantinople, he was very well educated and had expensive tastes. Combined, these two factors produced a brilliant king who lived in sumptuous surroundings. His scribe, known as Anonymous, wrote the earliest surviving chronicle of Hungarian history, *Gesta Ungarorum*. At the time, Hungary was enjoying an important role in international trade as it had ore and very fine livestock, horses, cattle and sheep. Unfortunately Béla's successor, András II, started selling off royal lands to the barons to finance his own pipedreams, and soon the nobles and the church rebelled. András was forced to sign the Golden Bull of 1222 guaranteeing the rights of the nobles – especially against the barons – and allowing them to interfere in royal matters if it appeared the king was endangering the health of the nation.

Marauding Mongols

András's son Béla IV might have been another great king, but the arrival of the Mongols consumed most of his energies. He defended Hungary as best he could, even allowing the heathen Cumans to settle in the country in exchange for military service (the Cuman towns and regions contain the syllable *kun* somewhere in the name). The main Mongol assault came in April 1241 near the village of Muhi, and it was devastating. But the king escaped and with his survival the country also survived. A year later the Mongols headed home and were never heard of again. Most of the great Hungarian fortresses were built after this time in expectation of another attack.

The Turkish Threat

The direct line of the Árpáds ended in 1301 with the death of András III, who had the sense to introduce a Diet for the nobles to counterbalance the barons' power. The latter finally elected Charles Robert of Anjou as king. He and his successors, Louis (Lajos) of Anjou and Sigismund of Luxemburg, who became Holy Roman Emperor, proved to be tough, just, and extremely shrewd. Their combined rule lasted from 1308 to 1437. They knew how to maintain the inner balance of power by playing the barons off against each other and against the nobles. They also steered a tight-rope course between Constantinople and Rome until the swelling Ottoman Empire upset the balance of power in the region.

The Turkish threat had made itself felt by the end of the 14th century, and as the decades wore on the attacks by this huge and well-equipped and trained army became more dangerous. János Hunyadi, Voivode of Transylvania, was able, thanks to a mercenary army, to deal a major blow against the Turks in 1456 at Nándorfehérvár (Belgrade); his son, Mátyás, who became King Mátyás Corvinus, also maintained an army of mercenaries to keep internal and external peace, notably by holding Austria in check. He ruled wisely and his Italian wife, Beatrix of Aragon, introduced the beauty and humanism of the Italian Renaissance to Gothic Hungary.

This peace and prosperity failed to outlive King Mátyás Corvinus. By the early 16th century the country was again being torn apart by internal strife. A peasant revolt led by Dózsa György was viciously crushed in 1514 and feudal servitude in perpetuity written into law. The Transylvanian Voivode Szapolyai and the Habsburg Emperor Ferdinand I, whose brother-in-law Ludwig had become King of Hungary, were both eyeing the throne.

On 29 August 1526, the king confronted the Turkish summer campaign at Mohács. The Hungarian army, far outnumbered, was massacred. For the Turks, under Suleiman II the Great, it was a footnote at the acme of their military and political power. For the Hungarians it was a major tragedy, for not only did the king die (drowned in a stream!), but the entire country fell apart. By the 1540s, the Turks occupied a large wedge of Hungary, including Pécs, Szeged, Buda and Esztergom. A strip of land in the west known as Royal Hungary stood as a buffer zone under the watchful eye of the Habsburgs. In the east, Transylvania cooperated with the Turks to remain independent.

The next 160 years proved a complex period of treaties and alliances, diplomatic and military moves between Turks, Habsburgs and Hungarians. Transylvania, however, grew into a major European power thanks to a number of able leaders, including István Báthori (1533–86), who also became king of Poland, and István Bocskai (1557–1606) and his freemen, the Hayducks, who provided him with an army feared by both Turks and Habsburgs.

Transylvania's decline began with the reign of György Rákóczi I from 1630 to 1648, and the catastrophic policies of his son and successor György Rákóczi II. The Habsburgs then decided to chase out the Turks and, under Eugene of Savoy, succeeded. Their subsequent occupation was so brutal, however, that the Hungarians still found the energy to go back to war spurred on by Ferenc Rákóczi II, Voivode of Transylvania. The enterprise petered out into the treaty of Szatmár in 1711, and Ferenc Rákóczi II fled to Turkey where he died in 1735. Hungary was in Habsburg hands.

Life with the Habsburgs

Hungary was exhausted in the 18th century. Vienna provided jobs and ballrooms for the nobles and the barons. The Habsburgs, especially the empress Maria Theresa, applied stick-and-carrot methods to their cantankerous subjects. Protestantism was discouraged. Artists and architects – Kracker, Dorfmeister, Maulbertsch, Carlone, Bergl – redid the country in Austrian baroque. Hungary's culture and language were threatened with extinction.

The Age of Enlightenment, however, ultimately had a revivifying effect. A small conspiracy under monk Ignác Martinovics failed, but a seed had been planted. By the 1830s a number of important people in Hungary were working toward a new birth of the nation, among others the poets Mihály Vörösmarty and Sándor Petőfi. Playwright József Katona had written *Bánk Bán*, a Hungarian epic later turned into an opera by Ferenc Erkel, who also composed the Hungarian national anthem to words by Ferenc Kölcsey. Count István Széchenyi, whose father had founded the Academy of Sciences in Budapest, was promoting industrial production (shipping on the Balaton, the chain-link bridge between Buda and Pest) and such institutions as the Academy of Sciences in Pest. Lajos Kossuth, a

Lajos Kossuth

lawyer, was promulgating more independence from Vienna. The Habsburg ruler Ferdinand I of Austria was fairly good-hearted, but seemed unaware of the tension.

The constellation was perfect for an explosion. Add economic troubles and another anti-monarchist spark from Paris, and you have the recipe for a revolution, which spread first to Vienna and then to Pest (Buda and Pest were separate cities at the time, and the Hungarian capital was Pozsony, today Bratislava in Slovakia). The revolution began with governmental and social reforms demanded by Lajos Kossuth on 15 March. Vienna agreed, a government was formed and all seemed well. But gradually anti-Habsburg voices became louder (including Kossuth's), and by September the moderate government of Batthyány resigned and full-scale war with Austria had broken out.

The Hungarians might have won, but the new emperor, Franz-Joseph I, requested and received Russian help. The 'Austrian' victory of August 1849 was followed by severe repression, which, owing to Austria's increasingly precarious international position, could not be maintained. After several major military defeats, notably against the Prussians in 1866 at Sadowa, Franz-Joseph I agreed to a compromise making him king of Hungary again, but granting the Hungarians a great deal of say in the (now) dual monarchy's governing.

The era of King and Kaiser following 1867 had all the outward trappings of a great society. Industry transformed the nation physically and economically, especially Budapest, which was declared the capital. However, the government was beset by a succession of scandals, while a growing proletariat became increasingly poor and despondent. The new Hungarian consciousness also alienated the numerous minorities. World War I, though temporarily serving as a rallying point, ultimately sounded the death knell of this gaudy time.

Budapest around 1900

War, Peace and Communism

The Trianon Treaty ending the war was signed on 4 June 1920. The two preceding years had witnessed a republic under the enlightened count Mihály Károlyi, an invasion by Romanians and Czechs, a communist state under Béla Kun, and the climb to power of Miklós Horthy, ironically an admiral in a landlocked country. Trianon was the cause of the two decades of national trauma that followed, because it hacked off two-thirds of Hungary's territory (including Transylvania, Slovakia and Croatia). As the country recovered financially from the war and then embarked on the roller-coaster ride of the international economic situation, the population began to feel they had been cheated. This feeling not only caused a sharp swing to the right, but ultimately pushed Hungary into the Nazi camp, because Hitler proffered bits of Slovakia in the first Vienna Award of November 1938, and bits of northern Transylvania in the second Award in 1940. In exchange, Hungary enacted anti-Jewish legislation and, when the time came, sent soldiers to fight with the Wehrmacht, notably in the Soviet Union and in Yugoslavia, where the Hungarians regained Croatia.

The Soviet star

As always in their history, the rulers of Hungary were not quite sure which horse they wanted to ride in World War II. The Allies were a better bet, but Hitler satisfied the national ego and the exactions of *realpolitik*. In March 1944 the Nazis finally occupied the country and installed a friendly government albeit still under Horthy. Eichmann also began dismantling Europe's last almost intact Jewish community, halted only partly by the commitment of Raoul Wallenberg, Swedish attaché, who saved tens of thousands of Jews by giving them neutral Swedish papers. His disappearance behind Soviet lines in January 1945 became a *cause célèbre*. Hungary's own home-grown Nazi party, the Arrow-Cross (Nyilas), also had a taste of power after the Germans physically removed Horthy in October 1944. By April 1945, however, the Nazis had been expelled from Hungary by the Red Army.

In the wake of the Soviet invasion came a host of communists who had gone into exile to Moscow during the 1920s and 1930s. Though by no means winning majorities during the first post-war elections, they did make their way into government from where they inveigled the rest of the left into an alliance. By 1948 they had consolidated their power with the help of the secret police, the ÁVO, later renamed ÁVH. Any potential opposition at the top was

Signing a treaty with Germany, 1990

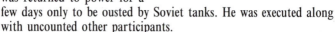

eradicated in the show trials of 1949. Collectivisation began in earnest, as did the arrest of anyone suspected of opposing the regime.

The gruesome years of communist control under Mátyás Rákósi began to thaw after Stalin's death in 1953. For a while Imre Nagy became Secretary General, ushering in an era of reform. General discontent resulted in a short-lived revolution that broke out on 23 October 1956, and lasted about 11 days. Nagy was returned to power for a few days only to be ousted by Soviet tanks. He was executed along with uncounted other participants.

János Kádár, who took the reins after 1956, was to be the last Hungarian dictator. He very gradually loosened the system, introducing what was to be nicknamed Goulash Communism. By the end of the 1960s he had already established limited private enterprise, and by the 1970s had opened the country to tourism. He maintained his allegiance to Moscow, even sending two divisions into Czechoslovakia in the Prague Spring of 1968, but he also had close ties with Austria. Increasing foreign debt, however, was the price of his policy to import more consumer items to Hungary.

The advent of *perestroika* in the USSR gave the signal for change in Hungary as well. Károly Grosz replaced Kádár in 1988, and was succeeded by Miklós Németh in 1989. Most of that year was spent forging the future at the round table with the MDF, at the time a loose opposition political alliance. In September, the government decided to let thousands of East German refugees leave: a floodgate had been opened that catalysed several revolutions in Czechoslovakia, East Germany and finally Romania.

Hungary's first free elections in March 1990 gave the opposition the most votes, but no majority or mandate. Meanwhile the Communists failed to cross the 5 percent mark. The years since have been marked by high inflation, high taxation, unemployment and social discontent. But as the 1990s progress, things are looking up. Foreign investment is high and optimism seems to be returning with Hungary's rapprochement with the European Community. Perhaps the biggest cloud on the horizon is Transylvania, where an ethnic minority of over 2 million continues to be the prey of chauvinist Hungarian leaders and Romanian *provocateurs*.

A sign of the times

Historical Highlights

2nd century AD The Romans reach the Danube and create the state of *Pannonia Inferior* in what is today western Hungary.

896 Árpád leads Magyar tribes into the Carpathian Basin.

955 The Magyar riders are defeated at the Lechfeld Battle.

1001 István I becomes the apostolic king of Hungary. He promulgates laws, creates counties and bishoprics.

1038 Death of István I.

1172–96 The reign of Béla III is a prosperous period. His scribe, Anonymous, writes *Gesta Ungarorum*, the earliest surviving chronicle of Hungary.

1222 András II signs the Golden Bull guaranteeing the rights of the nobles.

1241 Mongols defeat the Hungarians at Muhi.

1301 András III, the last in the direct line of the Árpád kings, dies.

1308 The barons elect Charles Robert of Anjou king of Hungary.

1456 János Hunyadi defeats the Turks at the siege of Nándorfehérvár (Belgrade).

1458 His son Mátyás (Corvinus) is crowned king, ushering in a Golden Age.

1526 The Hungarian army under Ludwig II is crushed by the Turks at the battle of Mohács.

1541 Buda is taken by the Turks. Hungary is divided into three parts, Royal and Turkish Hungary and Transylvania.

1571 István Báthori becomes Voivode of Transylvania endowing the region with the status of a European power.

1686–89 Hungary freed from the Turks by the Habsburg commander Eugene of Savoy.

1703 Ferenc Rákóczi II leads the Hungarians in an unsuccessful eight-year war against Habsburg domination.

1823 Sándor Petőfi, *né* Petrovics, Hungary's national poet, is born in Kiskőrös.

1830 Count Széchenyi begins organising Hungarian companies, the Danube Steamship Company and the Merchant (Kereskedelmi) Bank (1841).

1848–49 The revolution against Austrian supremacy headed by Kossuth ends in failure.

1867 Compromise with Austria creates the Austro-Hungarian Dual Monarchy.

1918–19 World War One and the monarchy end. Count Károlyi's republic fails in light of Romania's attack on Hungary. Béla Kun heads a communist state.

1920 The Treaty of Trianon reduces Hungary by two thirds. Admiral Horthy becomes Regent.

1938 and **1940** Hitler offers Slovakia and Transylvania in return for Hungarian cooperation.

1944 The Nazis are given a free hand in Hungary. On 15 October the Arrow-Cross movement takes power under Ferenc Szálasi.

1945 The Red Army occupies the country.

1949 The Communists take power; the Party is purged of Western influence in show trials.

1956 Revolution against the Soviet Union and communist rule is crushed by the Red Army.

1968 The New Economic Mechanism allows a limited free market to develop.

1990 First free elections to be held in Hungary. The Conservative Democratic Forum is the victor.

1996 The World Fair held in Budapest.

Day itinera

Budapest, Hungary's monolithic capital, is the most logical place to begin your visit. Several days can be spent at this bustling twin-centre city (Buda on the hill and Pest on the other side of the Danube) and in exploring destinations in all directions: the landscape and architectural treasures of the Danube Bend,

Expect the unexpected

wealthy Kecskemét, quaint Hollókö, the shores of Lake Balaton and the town of Győr. All are included in my Budapest itineraries.

I've then taken you through the western third of the country (as defined by the Danube), first along the western border itself to examine a string of towns: Szombathely, Kőszeg, Sopron, and Keszthely, all of which were ancient centres of trade between the Austrians and the Hungarians, before heading to Pécs in the balmy south of the country, where the Balkan breezes blow.

Having crossed the Danube, I then take you on a three-stage journey to the southeastern part of Hungary, including visits to the town of Szeged, the Southern Plain and the fabled region of Little Cumania.

The last section is devoted to the northeast of Hungary, to the Puszta or Great Plain and the foothills of the Carpathian Mountains. This region has a sleepy atmosphere, but most of Hungary's great reformers and reform movements were born here. Debrecen, the country's secret capital, was known as the Rome of Calvinism for its active espousal of the Protestant cause in the face of opposition from Budapest.

1. The Hungarian Capital

An early-morning stroll in the City Park, then through Budapest's Jewish Quarter to its main shopping street. Across the river up to the Castle District and Fishermen's Bastion.

Budapest awakes to the drone of traffic, the sibilant, clanking tramways and the cacophonous chatter of crowds. While the city goes through its matinal gymnastics, I propose you relax in the peace of the **City Park** (Városliget) to the northeast of the city centre at the far end of the Andrássy út and reachable either by bus or Underground. Have a dip in the **Széchenyi Baths** at Állatkerti körút 11, a grandiose, ornate neo-baroque (1909–13) building crowned by a giant green cupola. Thermal waters with a temperature of over 21°C (70°F) feed three outdoor pools, open all year.

Across from the entrance to the Széchenyi Baths is an odd collection of buildings, a baroque palace, a Romanesque church and the sullen walls and tower of a Transylvanian fortress. **Vajdahunyad**, as it is known, is in fact on an island in an artificial pond where one can boat in the summer and skate in the

Chess in the Széchenyi Baths

Heroes' Square

winter. The complex was originally designed by Ignác Alpár (1855–1928) for the millennial celebrations of the Hungarian state in 1896. It consists of replicas of great Hungarian works of architecture, including the church of Ják which lies to the left after entering. To the right, the cowled bronze figure opposite the entrance to the museum of agriculture is sculptor Miklós Ligeti's representation of Anonymous, the mysterious author of a 12th-century chronicle.

Walk out of the park into **Heroes' Square** (Hősök tere) immediately to the west, another by-product of Hungary's millennial celebrations. Visible from afar is the Archangel Gabriel standing atop a 36m (118ft) high column. At its foot are the seven tribal chiefs who led the Magyars into the Carpathian Basin back in 896, and the **Tomb of the Unknown Soldier**. In the background, two colonnades with statues of nine kings and five statesmen form a semicircle that embraces one end of the plaza.

The two neoclassical buildings flanking Heroes' Square are of considerable importance. To the right, when facing the column, is the **Exhibition Hall** (Műcsarnok). To the left is the **Hungarian Museum of Fine Arts** (Szépművészeti Múzeum), where you should spend at least an hour and a half browsing through the Antique Collection, the Egyptian Collection, the Graphic Arts Collection and the Esterházy Collection which includes Raphaels, Goyas and Rembrandts.

On leaving the museum turn right, cross Dózsa György út and find the entrance marked *földalatti* (meaning quite literally underground). This is Budapest's – and continental Europe's – first Underground line, the м1, which was opened in 1896. Catch a train to the stop marked **Opera**, where the splendid building by Miklós Ybl is just at the exit. It is usually open to visitors. Opposite is the **Drechsler House**, an early work by the art nouveau architect Ödön Lechner. Behind it, in the Paulay Ede u.

In the Jewish quarter

stands the newly renovated **Arany József Theatre**, a fine example of late art nouveau architecture.

Go right, take a left on Székely Mihály u. and then another right on Király u.. You are in the midst of the historic **Jewish quarter** of Budapest. The Gozsdu Udvár, a cross-block passage to Dob u.

on the left-hand side, is typical of the domestic life of the area. A little further is Rumbach Sebestyén u., where the synagogue (in Moorish style by the Viennese architect Otto Wagner) was recently cleansed of a thick layer of grime. Follow Rumbach u. straight to the **Great Synagogue**, which may be under restoration. It was built by another Viennese architect, Ludwig Forster, in the 1850s. The memorial to the victims of the Holocaust at the back of the synagogue, a metal weeping willow with the names of the victims written on the leaves, was created by Imre Várga.

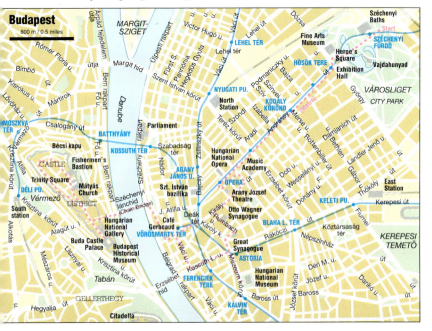

The Synagogue

The broad Károly körút at the synagogue takes you (towards the left) to the **Hungarian National Museum**, a neoclassical building in the centre of a small park on Múzeum körút. Its collection includes the royal crown and insignia, the very symbols of the Hungarian nation. Afterwards you can get a fairly inexpensive late lunch at the **Gösser söröző** (at the base of the Astoria Hotel), or grab a snack from a street vendor.

Váci u., off Kossuth L u., is Budapest's traditional shopping street. Its main claim to fame is its crowds, its shops, its lively tawdriness, its street vendors and performers, and its shabby moneychangers who should be avoided like the plague. It ends on **Vörösmarty tér** where shoals of portrait artists ply their trade, weather permitting. The square's erstwhile elegance has been compromised somewhat by the glassy building on the western flank. The statue of

The Gerbeaud, for elegant coffee

19th-century poet Mihály Vörösmarty stands in the middle surrounded by a cross-section of (Hungarian) listeners. Vörösmarty tér is also the site of the **Gerbeaud**, Budapest's oldest coffee house.

The **Danube** is just a few steps away at this point. Catch a cab on Apáczai Csere János u. across to the **Castle District** (the *várnegyed* in Hungarian), dominating the Buda side of the river. In 1987 this area was placed on UNESCO's Cultural Heritage list. The castle, at the southern end of the hill, has been repeatedly destroyed. It houses several museums, but at this point you will only have time to visit exhibitions in **Wing A**. Upstairs is the Ludwig modern art collection.

As you leave the museum, cross the yard by the great bronze of the *csikós* (Hungarian cow-puncher), pass the fountain by Alajos Stróbl depicting King Mátyás out hunting, and find the narrow passage leading to the front of the castle, where there is a terrace with a plunging view over Pest. The bronze rider here is Eugene of Savoy, who liberated the city from the Ottomans in 1686.

The Castle District, with its quiet streets, is ideal for a late-afternoon stroll. The neo-Gothic **Mátyás Church** and the **Fishermen's Bastion** (both by Frigyes Schulek) with the modern facade of the Hilton form an eclectic backdrop for musicians and street artists who gather here. Budapest's smallest coffee house, the **Ruszwurm**, is on Szentháromság u., which leads from the statue of the Trinity in front of the Mátyás Church. Further down the street is Toth Árpád sétány, a promenade along the western edge of the district.

To get back to Pest, return to the castle, catch the little funicular that goes down to Clark Ádám tér, and cross the **Széchenyi Bridge**. The promenade along the river is pleasant on warm evenings. For dinner, I suggest you try the **Bohémtanya**, Paulay Ede u. 6, just off Deák tér. It's often crowded, a very good sign.

Fishermen's Bastion

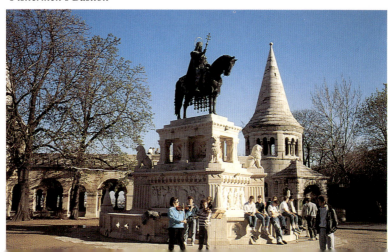

2. The Danube Bend

To the north of Budapest, the Danube Bend is only a small section of the 2,850km (1,770-mile) long river, beginning north of Szentendre and ending about 17km (11 miles) east of Esztergom. Its main attraction is the natural beauty of the landscape, which has been partly spoilt by the dam of Nagymaros.

Drive due north out of Budapest along Route 11 and the west bank of the Danube. After 20km (13 miles), you come to **Szentendre**, a pretty little town with narrow, tortuous streets and a pleasant, traffic-free centre. Park at designated spaces for visitors. Szentendre, meaning Saint Andrew, was nothing more than a humble village until the last decade of the 17th century, when Serb merchants settled here bringing wealth and the Greek Orthodox creed with them. The most beautiful of their four churches is the **Belgrade Cathedral**, with a prominent ox-blood red tower. It stands in the midst of a shady park surrounded by an ancient stone wall. Construction began in 1764 and was completed several decades later. The iconostasis inside the church, painted by Vasili Ostoic, is a superb baroque example of this art.

The Danube

The square yellow tower points the way to the Roman Catholic **Parish Church**. On the way, stop in at the studio of the impressionist painter Béla Czóbel (1883–1976). The interior of the church is pretty, but of greater interest, perhaps, is the little market that often besieges the surrounding square. The old stairways scaling the

Szentendre's Open-air Museum has a Greek Orthodox church

little hill on which it stands will ultimately take you to Fő tér, **Main Square**, the centre of town, which is marked by a highly decorated cross of wrought iron standing on a red marble column. Erected in 1763, it serves as a reminder of the Serbs who were given rights here. Just off the square you will find Görög u. and the **Gallery of Margit Kovács** (1902–77), who worked porcelain into touching figures. Craft-mongers also keep the flag of mercantilism flying in town. A few locals have spiffed up their old carts and offer horse-and-buggy rides around the main sights.

If the weather is hot, buy a bottle of water before visiting the **Open-air Village Museum** (*Skanzen*), which lies a few miles away on the northwestern edge of the town along the road to **Pilisszentlászló**. Its houses were garnered from various parts of the country. Not to be missed, for it is a little out of the way, is the 17th-century wooden Greek Orthodox church from the village of

Mándok near Zahony on the Ukrainian border. It has beautifully carved and coloured furnishings. If you want a break for lunch, in the grounds is a homey restaurant serving basic Hungarian food.

The first afternoon stop is **Visegrád**, 23km (14miles) to the north, which is at the heart of the Danube Bend. Not much is left of the huge fortified complex with countless rooms, gardens and fountains where King Mátyás once held court. The ruins up near the Hotel Silvanus, a detour of about 20 minutes, merit a visit if only to muse on the evanescence of material things and to take in the striking view of the Bend and the Börzsöny Mountains beyond.

Much praise has been heaped on **Esztergom**, the final stop for the day. It was once the residence of Hungarian kings from István I, who was allegedly born here, to Béla IV (1235–70). Secondly it boasts Christianity's earliest basilica, the **Cathedral of the Assumption**, although the current construction bearing that name is of more recent date. Building started in 1822 and continued into the 1860s; resemblance to St Peter's in Rome is not coincidental. The cupola supported by 24 pillars is over 90m (300ft) high and beckons to the faithful for miles around. And yet, in spite of manifest pomp, the basilica is a sober affair: the dominant colour is stone grey, which neatly high-

lights the paintings inside (copies of Titian among others). The
Bakócz Chapel off to one side is a Renaissance relic from the previous basilica. Note, too, the figure of Bishop Pázmány casting his
gaze over the pews; he was one of the few shepherds sent in by the
Habsburgs who attempted to re-catholicise the country without
bleeding it dry at the same time. Reliquaries, ceremonial attire,
chalices and other church paraphernalia have been gathered in a

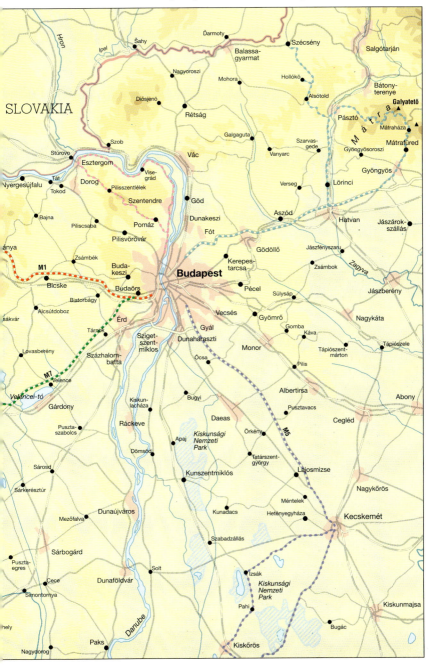

Cathedral dome, Esztergom

treasure chamber which is accessible from the transept.

The remains of the **Old Castle** on the western flank of the basilica house more secular exhibits, including an ancient living-room, a Renaissance room where Bishop János Vitéz once worked, and the room of Beatrix, queen and wife of King Mátyás. Finally, at the foot of the hill, to the right of the Vízivárosi (Water Town) Church, is a fine collection of Christian art culled from Hungarian, Austrian and German churches. Follow that with a comfortable stroll into town where you might either stop for an early dinner or just a refreshment. A good, fairly cheap place is the **Kispipa étterem**, where one should try a fish speciality from the Danube. Return to Budapest over the Pilis Hills (follow signs for Pilisszenlélek).

3. Sights along the M1

The charming towns of Zsámbék, Tata and Győr lie to the west of Budapest.

About 12km (7 miles) west of Budapest on the M1 is **Zsámbék**, a village of about 4,000 inhabitants lying in the foothills of the Gerecse Mountains. Its most famous sight is the dramatic ruin of a 13th-century basilica once run by the Premonstratensian order and later by the Pauline monks. It once consisted of a high nave flanked by two smaller ones but, after barely surviving the Turks and the Habsburg reconquest, it suffered a major earthquake in 1763.

Zsámbék also has a Turkish fountain in its centre, but you should not miss the **Lamp Museum**, which has been arranged in a typical Hungarian farmhouse (on the way to Páty). The collection covers mainly the 19th and early 20th century and includes such items as a Chinese vase heretically turned into a petrol lamp and a Soviet-conceived gas lamp-cum-generator.

Three exits later on the M1 comes **Vértesszőlős** where archaeologists discovered a half-million year old settlement of *homo archanthropus*.

An organ grinder plies his trade

The **Open-air Museum** is on the right. A couple of miles up the road lies **Tata**, where you may start by visiting the **Ethnographical Museum**, located at Ady Endre út 24 in what was once a water mill, the Miklós Mill. The museum is devoted to the life, times and household items of the Danube Swabians, as they were called, people mainly from Swabia and Alsace (that is, German-speaking) who migrated to Hungary after the Turkish wars. The mill was designed by a proud architect from their ranks, Jakob Fellner (1722–80).

Ady Endre út runs into Országgyűlés tér, easily recognisable by the curious hexagonal clock-tower on the right. Turn left at the church into Béla Bartók u..

On the left comes the 18th-century Nepomuk Mill, 90m (300ft) further is the Cifra (fancy) Mill, and finally the **Tata Castle** which is surrounded by a moat. The castle's origins stretch back to even before the days of Sigismund of Luxemburg (1387–1437), who made Tata a residence. Later, King Mátyás brought his opulent taste to bear on its furnishings and on

Bay window, Xantus János Múzeum

the life behind its stark walls. A tall, green tile stove documents his stay. Among its other exhibits is a collection of historical artifacts, old-fashioned weapons, a billiard table and regional products.

Tata is a half-hour drive from the ancient bishopric of **Győr** on the M1, so lunch can be taken at either place.

Only Győr's majestic neo-baroque **Town Hall** on the left, with its tall tower, hints at something other than a depressing industrial landscape beyond the motorway. Turn right wherever you read the sign 'Centrum', on the Czuczor G. u. for example, park the car and find Széchenyi tér, the old town centre and **market-place**. The two dominant features here are the Marian statue and the Church of St Ignatius, both of which are baroque. The church boasts frescos by Paul Tröger, the great Viennese painter and teacher, whose students introduced the rococo style. On the other side of the square is the **Xantus János Múzeum** which displays a variety of collections from ethnographic to numismatic. This baroque construction has a remarkable bay window with a crucifixion scene forming the central post and lintel of the two windows.

The Jedlik Ányos u. leaves Széchenyi Square to the north. Just before the bridge take a left into Gutenberg tér. The strange statue here was designed by Fischer von Erlach. It was a present from Emperor Charles III to beg forgiveness for the excessive zeal of an Austrian soldier, who broke a monstrance carried in a procession when he tried to arrest a suspected deserter.

Head next for the **Cathedral of Our Dear Lady** on Martinovits

Shop sign

tér. Long gone are the days when a simple Romanesque church stood here. A Gothic church replaced it in the 15th century, the Turks used it as an arsenal in the 17th century and then destroyed it, and Bishop Draskovich had the present structure erected in the 17th century. In the following century Anton Maulbertsch painted the ceiling frescos.

Behind the cathedral you can walk along the bastions that preside over the confluence of the Little (Moson) Danube and the Rába. Then walk down toward the **Carmelite Church** which stands in pleasant surroundings on the 'Square of the Republic', now called Vienna Gate Square, adjacent to the Rába. Constructed between 1721–25, the magnificent baroque facade and interior were the work of Martin Witwer. The erstwhile Carmelite monastery beside the church is now a very pleasant hotel. Walk along it and turn left on the Virágpiác (Flower Market): Kazinczy u. is straight ahead and takes you back to Széchenyi Square.

Should time and light allow, drive the 20km (13 miles) southward to **Pannonhalma**, a Benedictine abbey on top of a small hill. Its appearance is 19th-century, but its interior reveals medieval elements, a Gothic columned courtyard with a vaulted ceiling, a venerable old library, a coin collection and a beautiful church.

For dinner, either return to Győr or try the **motorway restaurant** at kilometre 83 on the way back to Budapest. The food is simple, but the house is one of those atavistic creations of the foremost Hungarian architect Imre Makovec.

The Carmelite Church and the Rába

A tour of Hungary's first capital; then on via Veszprém to Lake Balaton, the country's main tourist attraction. Enjoy a fish supper after some Indian poetry in Balatonfüred.

Székesfehérvár lies 66km (40 miles) southwest of Budapest just off the M7 motorway. From the looks of the place, the fact that it is one of the oldest and most illustrious of Hungarian towns may seem absurd at first. Yet it was Hungary's first capital, chosen by Géza himself and later inherited by István I. Thirty-seven kings were anointed here, 17 buried in a mighty basilica that exists only as a stone pattern in the grounds behind the Bishop's Palace. The Turks used it as an arsenal and it appears to have blown up in 1601. The lapidarium here gives only the vaguest idea of what Székesfehérvár might once have looked like. Its most prestigious item is a sarcophagus which allegedly held the remains of István I himself. A flood, however, washed them away, along with the remains of his 16 colleagues.

Plan to arrive early, around 9am, and park near the northern end of the old town (belváros), Dózsa György tér or Országzászló tér. Stroll down Marcius 15. u., the aorta of Székesfehérvár. On the right at Várkapu u. is a statue of **György Varkocs**, a general who held off the Turks during the 1543 campaign. About 45m (150ft) further, on the left, is the **Fekete Sas** (Black Eagle) **Patika**, an old apothecary-turned-museum. The city's most important **museum**, however, is diagonally opposite, adjacent to the Cistercian

'Black Eagle' Museum

church; but it opens at 10am, so I suggest you visit it on the way back. The museum displays numerous relics from the town's history, including Roman sculptures and gravestones, culled from the large settlement outside the nearby village of Tác. Upstairs you will find fine collections of Avar, Celtic and Slav jewellery and pottery, and exhibits from Hungarian history.

Marcius 15. u. runs into Szabadság tér. To the left is the **Bishop's Palace** mentioned above, a sober classical building. To the right is a **Franciscan Church** and cloister, as the effigy of the little friar standing in the niche suggests. The **Town Hall**, straight ahead, dates from the early 18th century. The equestrian statue in front is some martial memorial to a regiment of hussars, but the fountain surmounted by a round stone supported by three feline creatures has become one of the symbols of Székesfehérvár. The **Apple of the Nation**, as it is called (Országalma), was designed by a sculptor named Béla Ohmann and represents the historic importance of the town as consecrated by King István I.

Szent-István Cathedral

Walk along the side of the Franciscan church to the **Hiermer House**, which in spite of its fame as a rococo gem is quite run-down. Then turn left along Liszt Ferenc u. and proceed to the little stairway that leads up to Csók István u. The **Szent-István Cathedral**, with its two majestic towers, comes into view. To its left is the Chapel of St Anne, which the Turks used as a prayer room. It is one of the sole survivors of medieval Székesfehérvár.

It takes about 35 minutes on Route 8 to reach **Veszprém**, one of Hungary's oldest bishoprics, whose first cathedral and castle were built as long ago as the 9th century. The protected **Castle Quarter** is clustered around a single street out on a spur overlooking the town. The mostly 18th-century houses and churches here have all been restored to perfection. Behind the entrance stands the pretty **Fire Tower**, completed in 1817. There are three churches, all well worth a peek inside: the Piarist (teaching institute) is the first on the right. The Franciscan church stands on the main square in whose centre is an elaborate representation of the Trinity. The house almost opposite is the baroque **Bishop's Palace**, a work by Jakob Fellner. Adjacent to it is a little chapel honouring Gizella, the wife of King István. The royal couple are honoured in two statues at the end of the street. The third church, notable for its two towers, is the **Cathedral of St Michael** (Szent Mihály).

The next stop on the day's outing is **Tihany**, a peninsula in **Lake Balaton**, which is mostly a nature preserve with interesting waterfowl. Here the **Belső-tó**, or interior lake, is higher than and unconnected with the Balaton. But most come to visit the **Abbey** at the top of the hill at Tihany, which was founded by the Benedictines in 1055 and became the lonely burial place of András I in 1060. Parts of the original church remain below the current 18th-century abbey.

The last stop of the day is **Balatonfüred**, which you bypassed on the way to Tihany. The dignified houses at the centre recall less gaudy days in 'füred. The promenade along the lake has been named after Rabindranath Tagore, the Indian poet, who was a frequent visitor. He (like a number of other illuminati from politics, science and literature, including Edward Teller, Rajhiv and Indira Gandhi) planted a tree here, and a marble stone inscribed in English and Hungarian with one of his poems was placed before it with the lines (*sic*):

The lakeside at Balatonfüred

When I'm no longer on this earth my tree,
Leth the ever-renewed leaves of thy spring,
Murmur to the wayfarer:
The poet did love while he lived.

For supper, I suggest you try the **Halászkert** on Széchenyi tér, which specialises in fish. Give *fogas* a try, a type of pike-perch found only in the Balaton and much praised by culinary experts.

5. Kecskemét and the Puszta

Kecskemét is famed for its schnapps; Kiskőrös is the birthplace of Hungary's national poet Sándor Petőfi. Lunch in a traditional restaurant amongst the horsemen of the Great Plain or Puszta.

Kecskemét lies on the sandy flatlands southeast of Budapest that form the western edge of Hungary's famous Great Plain, referred to generally as the Puszta. The soil around the town is ideal for growing fruit, especially peaches, apricots and grapes. Today, Kecskemét is best known for its schnapps, particularly *barack* (pronounced 'borrotsk') *pálinka*.

The town is an hour's drive from Budapest on the M5. Begin at **Széchenyi tér**, squeezed between the Arany Homok (Golden Sands) Hotel and a flight of houses with typically Hungarian art nouveau ornaments, one serving as a cinema (*mozi*). Of note here is the small but very pretty **Greek Orthodox Church**, built in 1829. Széchenyi Square opens into a broad, tree-shadowed plaza: Kossuth Square and the adjacent Szabadság Square. The church to the right is the **Catholic Great Church** (Nagytemplom), a standard example of the sober late-baroque style in Hungary. The large brick-red building beside it is the **Town Hall**, an art nouveau creation by Ödön Lechner and Gyula Partos, decorated with

Kecskemét's art nouveau town hall

the coat-of-arms of the town which shows a goat (*kecske* in Hungarian). The carillon over the entrance plays a little folk song at 12.05pm, 6.05pm and 8.05pm.

Before continuing anti-clockwise around the square, make a detour to the **Theatre**, which is visible from the town hall. Designed by the ubiquitous Ferdinand Fellner and Hermann Helmer, it was named after József Katona (1791–1830), who was born in Kecskemét. His most famous work is *Bánk Bán*, which, set to music by Ferenc Erkel, became Hungary's national opera.

Back on Kossuth Square, you will pass **St Michael's Church** on your right, an ancient church indeed (13th century), but entirely redone in baroque style by the Franciscans. Perhaps more interesting than the interior is the finely carved calvary in front of the church. The neighbouring church belongs to the Protestants; it, too, was rebuilt during the late 18th century. And beside that stands an exotic-looking building that once belonged to the Franciscans, but was turned into the Zoltán Kodaly Music Institute. Kodaly, composer and musical ethnographer, was born in Kecskemét.

Next is the **Cifra palota** (adorned palace), designed by Géza Markus in Hungarian art nouveau style and decorated with colourful panels from the Zsolnay factory in Pécs. The 'palace' has an exhibition of Hungarian paintings. On the other side of Rákóczi út is the **Synagogue**, a splendid example of the Romantic-Moorish style in Hungary. It has served as the House of Science and Technology for some time now. The stained-glass windows and copies of Michelangelo statues on show in the foyer should be on your list of sights.

Performing on the Puszta

The last side of the square is for devotees of shipping rather than for sightseers. The office of **Pusztatourist** is here, where you can find out when horsemen will be showing their skills in nearby Bugác (*see below*), in the Kiskunság National Park, or in Lajosmizse. These shows often come with a lunch at a *csárda*, a traditional restaurant with whitewashed walls, red tablecloths, long wooden tables, and waiters who smell a little of hay. The food is often also red and spicy, seldom for vegetarians, and at times feels like one of the horses' hoofs in one's stomach. But the general ambience is terrific.

Bugác, off Route 54 south of Kecskemét, has an open-air museum displaying grey longhorn cattle, Racka sheep (with twisted horns), as well as the woolly Mangalitza pigs, whose meat is supposed to be far superior to that of the garden-variety pig. As for the equestrian shows, they run the gamut from the ox cart to whip-cracking, standing on the backs of two horses. It is undoubtedly show biz, but there is a lot of skill and tradition involved.

After the show, continue south on Route 54 and then west on 53

The birthplace of Sándor Petrovics

through vineyards to **Soltvadkert** (it has a lake) and **Kiskőrös**, which is well known to most Hungarians. It is here that Hungary's national poet was born in 1823: Sándor Petőfi, *né* Petrovics. He moved around quite a bit as a child, became an actor, published an anthology of poetry, and, in 1848, played a major role in spurring on the revolutionary spirit of Hungarians against the Habsburgs (*Talpra Magyar*, 'Rise up Hungarians', was his famous poem read out in March 1848). He participated actively as a soldier, became a captain, and allegedly died at Segesvár (now in Romania) in a rout at the hand of the Russian interventionist army. The house where he was born stands on the main square appropriately called **Petőfi tér**. It is typical of many simple Hungarian homes, with its three rooms, kitchen in the middle, and low thatched roof. One of the rooms has furnishings belonging to the family, another displays documents relating to them. The bust of Petőfi in the garden is the oldest in Hungary (1861). A statuary of Petőfi's translators has been arranged in the rear garden.

Return to Kecskemét via Pahi and Izsák. On the way into town is a typical *csárda* on the left-hand side of the road, where they serve excellent *pörkölt*s (what we know as *goulash*).

6. Mountains and a Gem of a Village

To Hollókő, with its quaint houses, and lunch from the local Palozan menu. On to Forgách Castle and then return to Budapest over the scenic Matra Mountains.

Your main destination today is a little village in the Cserhát Mountains to the northeast of Budapest. Leave the capital on Route 30 heading east, through the attractive baroque towns of Gödöllő and Aszód, and then head north for 30km (19 miles) along Route 21 up the broad Zagyva Valley, until you reach the turn-off on the left. A short drive through Alsótold and Felsőtold will bring you to another left turn leading to one of the gems of northern Hungary: **Hollókő** is on UNESCO's World Heritage List, but unless you penetrate the elongated village far enough to reach the old part you will never know why. The street is flanked with brilliant white houses, each one

In the old village

Restored facade of Forgách Castle

prettier than the next, whose occupants are mostly elderly Palozan women dressed in traditional costume. The Palozans, who are of Slav origin, are thought to have settled in northern Hungary around the 11th or 12th centuries. The plain, picturesque **Church** with a wooden bell tower standing at the street's fork, is somewhat corny on the inside. The **Museum,** giving information on the life and folk art of the Palozans, is on the left after the church. A little further is a house selling handicrafts, although no doubt the ladies of Hollókö will already have offered you embroidered handkerchiefs and book-marks.

Have a lunch of Palozan specialities (the soup is the most famous) before driving north to **Szécsény** (16km/10 miles), to visit the beautifully restored **Forgách Castle**. It was built in the late 17th century from the stones of the local fortress of which little remains but walls and dispersed bastions. The castle's great moment came in 1705 when Ferenc Rákóczi II chose Szcécsény as the location for a national Diet of independent Hungary. A hunting museum has been arranged on the first floor, and the carriage house on the right has a fascinating little museum dedicated to Sándor Csoma Körösi, an orientalist who edited the first Tibetan grammar (1834).

Into the hills

To return to Budapest via Gyöngyös, I suggest you take the scenic route, which involves following the winding mountain road along the picturesque **Matra Mountains** eastwards from **Pásztó**. It first leads up hill and down dale to the **Galyatetö** (Hungary's second highest peak). Parking spaces are often strategically located for the best views, and some even have mountain maps giving the names and heights of peaks. A little further on, at the other side of Route 24, is the **Kékestetö**, the Blue Roof, Hungary's highest summit (1,015m/3,330ft). The top itself is occupied by an egregious television tower, but the view and the fresh air attracts throngs, catered for by numerous snack-mongers.

7. Szombathely and Ják

Szombathely's sights include a temple to the Egyptian goddess Isis, and the nearby village of Ják is famed for its Romanesque church. An open-air museum reveals aspects of local rural life.

Roman stone, Szombathely

Szombathely, the capital of Vas county, is situated in the far west of the country just before the Austrian border, about 220km (136 miles) from Budapest. The name literally means Saturday Place, and implies that once upon a time a market was held here on that day. The Romans under Emperor Claudius settled the area in the first century AD and called their town *Savaria*. Its most famous son was St Martin of Tours,

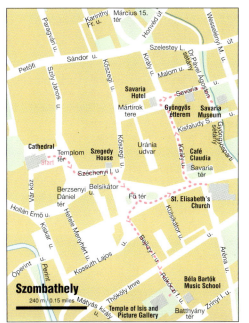

Szombathely
240 m / 0.15 miles

the patron saint of France, born here around AD316. Szombathely went through Hungarian history with the usual damage, though not so much from the Turks as from rebel Hungarians trying to snatch it from the Habsburgs. Today the Austrians are there again, usually buying everything that is for sale and filling the cafés to the brim.

Parking is generally available close to the **Cathedral**, an austere, grey church with two towers that you should visit first. It suffered a bombardment on 4 March 1945, which explains the un-baroque features of its interior. The focus of the decoration are the paintings in the side-altars. The most valuable are the Dorfmeister in the second to the right, depicting St István, and the two Maulbertsch paintings at the ends of the transept. At the back of the cathedral is a garden of Roman ruins, discovered in 1938. The Bishop's Palace to the left of the church entrance opens a little later and has

a noteworthy display of ecclesiastical attire and paraphernalia. István Dorfmeister painted the frescos in the entrance room, which also contains antique carved stones that have been placed strategically in front of the paintings.

Cross the main street Szily J u. and walk to Fő tér, the commercial hub of the town. Turn right and head down Bejczy I u. and II Rákóczi Ferenc u. to the next two sights (they open at 10am): on the left is the **Synagogue**, built by Ludwig Schöne in 1881, and serving today as a recital hall for the Béla Bartók music school; to the right is the **Isäum**, a reconstructed temple devoted to the goddess Isis, dating to the end of the 2nd century. The ghastly greyish-white building in the background that looks as if it's about to take off is the **Szombathely Picture Gallery**. It contains valuable collections, notably the one celebrating the age of Activism in

The Isäum, or Temple of Isis

Hungary in the 1920s and 1930s. One of the main exponents is Gyula Derkovits (1894–1934) who provides a poignant, humorous, look at everyday life in his day: barge-pullers on the Danube, two shadows overwhelmed by a bow, or the self-portraits with beard, without beard, with a sneer and with a look of amazement.

On leaving the gallery, return to the centre of town and take a right on Fő tér. It leads to Savaria tér, where you will find on the right the **Szt Erzsébet Church**, which boasts early baroque furnishings. Opposite, on the corner of Bajcsi-Zsilinski u., is the **Café Claudia**. If you want a coffee and it is too full, an alternative is the **Savaria Hotel** down Bajcsi-Zs u.. Its 10m (30ft) high dining-room is very impressive.

Savaria u. begins at the hotel as well, and goes right by the **Savaria Museum**, a dignified old building in the midst of a small park. The basement has a sizeable collection of Roman stones. The

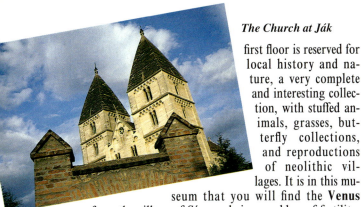

The Church at Ják

first floor is reserved for local history and nature, a very complete and interesting collection, with stuffed animals, grasses, butterfly collections, and reproductions of neolithic villages. It is in this museum that you will find the **Venus** from the village of Sé, an obvious goddess of fertility, judging from the prominence of her lower abdomen and thighs. On the way to the museum you may have noticed the **Gyöngyös étterem**, which serves light meals.

It's time to get back to the car and drive out to **Ják** to the southwest. Follow signs for Körmend, and 200m (650ft) after the Aral petrol station at the exit of town, turn right. Ten minutes later you will arrive in Ják whose only claim to fame is the Romanesque **Church**, whose two square towers dominate the skyline. The portal, a series of concentric arches adorned by the figures of Christ and the 12 apostles, is particularly beautiful. If you visited Vajdahunyad in Budapest where a replica stands (*see Itinerary 1*), it will already be familiar.

Ják, a Benedictine abbey, was begun in the year 1214 by its sponsor Márton of Ják. It was completed in 1256, destroyed during the Turkish wars, redone in baroque style, and finally, at the turn of the 20th century, restored to its original form by Frigyes Schulek, the architect of the Fishermen's Bastion and the Mátyás Church in Budapest. Unfortunately, few of the original frescos remain.

Enough time should be left to get back to Szombathely and to visit the open-air museum off **Béla Bartók körút** (stay on the Körmend road and turn left at the stadium). Typical farmhouses from the region have been gathered here and furnished with authentic gardening and agricultural implements, rustic furniture, pots, pans, crockery, and furniture. Tonight have dinner at the **Kispiter Csárda** on Szombathely's Mátyás Király u.. It specialises in fish.

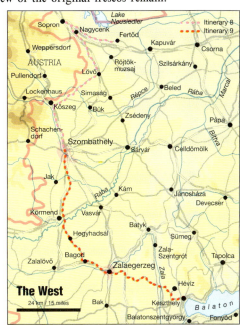

From Kőszeg, where Captain Jurisics once defied the Turks, to Sopron, whose old town has an extraordinary concentration of historic monuments. Crown the day with a visit to the 'Versailles of Hungary' near Fertőd.

It is only 16km (10 miles) from Szombathely to **Kőszeg**, a compact town of 11,000 inhabitants in the shadow of low mountains. The main square, with the baroque column (1712) supporting a representation of the Holy Trinity and the slender spires of the **Church of Jesus's Heart** in the background, is so attractive that the first-time visitor might think that was enough and leave.

But follow Várkör to the right of the church till you come to the **Castle**. Its great moment came in August 1532 when Captain Miklós Jurisics (a Croatian nobleman) held off a vastly superior Turkish army, thus preventing an attack on Vienna. Today the castle has several exhibitions of local history and local culture (see the furniture on the first floor) and a lapidarium.

Go straight out of the front entrance (you

Heroes' Gate

sneaked in through the back) and take a right on Rájnis József u.. There are two churches here. First is **Szent Jakab** (St James), built around 1400, but redone in baroque style by the Jesuits in the 1750s. Two of Captain Jurisics's children, who died of the plague, are buried here. The second church, **Szt Imre** (St Emmerich), was completed in 1618 and boasts a Dorfmeister painting over the altar. On Jurisics tér, at the end of Rájnis J u., trees cast a pleasant shade over the Marian statue and the town well. The **Town Hall**, dating from the early 18th century, is beautifully decorated with Hungary's, Jurisics's and Kőszeg's coats-of-arms, and religious motifs. Opposite is the **Sgraffitto House**, built and decorated in the 17th century. **Heroes' Gate**, which dates to 1932, takes you back to the main square.

If you leave Kőszeg around 11am, you can make it to **Sopron** in Hungary's far northwestern corner by noon, and even stop by the **Széchenyi Castle** in Nagycenk on the way. It is a hotel today but does have a small museum dedicated to Széchenyi, one of Hungary's greatest personalities during the 19th century. When

Sopron's Fire Tower

Stained glass, Storno House

arriving in Sopron, try to park on the peripheral road near the 600-year-old **Fire Tower**, easily identifiable from its columned gallery topped by an onion dome. That is where you will find the old town of Sopron, called *Scarbantia* by the Romans and *Ödenburg* by the Germans. Enter through the **Elökapu** (front gate) under the tower, which can be climbed. The street then proceeds alongside the Town Hall to **Fő tér** (main square).

Now's the time for a snack at the **Generális** restaurant. Sitting outside allows for an overview: to the right is a typical baroque statue of the Trinity. Behind it is the former Benedictine church known as the **Goat Church** (Kecske-templom), because the sponsoring family's coat-of-arms featured a goat. Ahead is the **Gambrinus House** (a café), which stands on Gothic and Renaissance foundations, and has a patisserie exhibition.

The place to start your exploration of Sopron, however, is the **Storno House** next to the Generális. It consists of two floors of museums. The first is devoted to the life and times of Sopron. The second floor is the richly decorated apartment of Franz Storno the elder, a painter, art collector and local chimney-sweeping master. The house on the other side of the Generális, known as the **Fabricius House**, has a collection of carved stones culled from several centuries of Sopron history.

To visit the rest of the old town, go past the Goat Church and along the Templom u.. The blue house with the Madonna in an alcove over the *porte-cochère* (vehicle entrance) houses a **Mining Museum**. A little further along next to the church is a small museum documenting the trials and tribulations of Sopron's Protestants. Take Fegyvertár u. left to Orsolya tér (Ursula Square), thus named after the neo-Gothic church standing there which is owned and operated by the Ursuline order. The house directly opposite with the arcade on the ground floor dates from 1570.

Proceed now down Új u.. At No 22 is a medieval **Synagogue**, restored, at No 11 is another one unrestored (you have to look for it). Új u. 16 is a skilfully modernised **Gothic House**, and opposite is a baroque-ised 15th-century house decorated with sgraffito. Turn the corner at the Gambrinus and go back to Orsolya tér on Szt György u.. Every house here has a little plaque describing its origin: on the right are the Eggenberg House, the Protestant convent

and the Erdődy palace, the latter newly renovated. The main building on the left is the **Church of St George** (Szt György templom).

Make sure you leave Sopron by about 3pm to make the final sight of the day, about 30km (19 miles) east of town on the Kapuvár-Győr road near the village of **Fertőd**. This was where Count Miklós (Nicholas) Esterházy chose to build his summer residence, known today as the **Versailles of Hungary**. It was built between 1764 and 1766, consists of over 120 rooms and endless gardens wrested from surrounding swamps. It had a little theatre, too, and Esterházy's private composer was none other than Joseph Haydn. The rooms are a catalogue of the taste of the time, some draped in chinoiserie, others decorated with flowery stucco (the Sala Terrena); the master bedroom is surprisingly sober.

9. The Road to Keszthely

Keszthely, one of Balaton's nicest towns, and a cultural centre in Hungary in its own right, is easily accessible from Szombathely. Set off early to take in more sights on the way.

Nineteen kilometres (11 miles) south of Szombathely on Route 86 is **Körmend**, where the Batthyány family, major role-players in Hungarian history, kept an estate. The palace is a baroque affair containing remains of the fortifications of its 14th-century predecessor. Except for a small museum, it is not open to the public, but you can take a morning stroll through the surrounding arbour.

Thirty kilometres (18 miles) further down Route 76 comes **Zalaegerszeg**, the capital of Zala county. The town has some surprising treasures in store: watch for what looks like an oil derrick on the left, a few hundred metres after entering the outskirts. The next road to the left will take you to an **Open-air Museum** presenting typical peasant houses of the Göcsej, the name of the local region. Right next to this idyllic reconstruction of Hungarian peasant life is a museum devoted to the Hungarian oil industry.

Parking in the centre can be found on the right in front of the old Arany Bárány (Golden Sheep) Hotel. The large street to the left leads to the **Göcseji Museum**. Its first floor concentrates on local history, and is a good complement to the open-air museum seen earlier. Here you will find displays covering everything from jewellery by the Avars and Celts to hunting exhibits. On the ground floor is an exhibition devoted to **Zsigmond Kisfaludi Strobl** (1884–1975), one of Hungary's foremost sculptors.

If you leave Zalaegerszeg at around 1pm, you should arrive in Keszthely by 2pm. The road there twists and turns through pleasant, hilly countryside. Drive through **Hévíz**, which features one of the most remarkable natural phenomena of Hungary: a giant hotwater lake. Changing rooms and indoor pools have been built on stilts and look rather mysterious with their sharp spires.

Hévíz lotus

But on to **Keszthely**, whose main sight is well marked, the **Castle of Count Festetics**, the town's ruling dynasty since 1737. Parking is available at the main gate. The central section was begun by Kristóf Festetics in 1745. His son Pál had the two wings attached in 1770, and his son György, in turn, enlarged it, and being a member of Hungary's class of enlightened aristocrats, created a **Library** that remains one of the finest collections of ancient books in Hungary to this day. He also founded Europe's first agricultural college, the neighbouring **Georgikon**, which operated between 1797 and 1848 and can be visited after the castle (it has an interesting display of farming machinery and tools). First, however, visit the chambers of the Festetics on the first floor of the castle, with their valuable collection of furniture and furnishings from the 18th and 19th centuries.

Head back into the town centre, and stroll down the main drag, Kossuth u., a pedestrian precinct with shops, restaurants, bars. **No 22**, on the left, is the oldest house in town, and was the birthplace of the famous Karl Goldmark, violinist and composer. A little further is a restaurant with folkloric shows (a major concession to the highly touristy atmosphere of the place). The **Great Church** on the main square (Fő tér) is, like most churches in Hungary, of Gothic origin but redone in baroque. Some gravestones of red and black marble have survived the restoration, and beside the church you will find a garden of ruins, left over from Keszthely's past.

You can either stay in Keszthely for the evening, take a trip on the lake, or return to Hévíz again for a swim and a fine meal.

Lake Balaton near Keszthely

the South

10. Pécs

The Romans and Turks loved the town of Pécs for its almost Mediterranean climate; the Habsburgs liked it for the easy booty it provided. Modern travellers enjoy the town for its pleasant balance of amenities, good hotels, cultural events, museums, and the slightly exotic air it exudes.

Next to Eger (*see Itinerary 17*), Pécs is the most Turkish town in Hungary, with one still-functioning mosque. This city of 180,000 lies about 200km (125 miles) south of Budapest, at the foot of the Mecsek Hills, which drop on to the dry plain of the Dráva, a river separating Hungary from Croatia.

The 'mosque' church and Holy Trinity statue

Begin your tour at **Széchenyi tér**, specifically at the doors of the **Catholic Church**, which was once the Djami of Pasha Gasi Kassim. The giant dome dates only from the 1950s, when the authorities finally decided to restore the mosque's original look. Islamic elements include the ogee arches over the windows and Koranic inscriptions on the walls inside. The odd positioning of the church is due to its facing Mecca. The plaza in front of it hints at other episodes of Hungarian history: the statue of the Holy Trinity recalls the baroque age dominated by the Austrians, and the equestrian statue of János Hunyadi, coyly standing off to the eastern side of the square, suggests the glorious days of the mid-15th century, when the Turks still appeared to be defeatable.

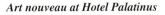

Art nouveau at Hotel Palatinus

The houses around Széchenyi tér are all under protection. On the western flank is the erstwhile **Pécs Savings Bank** (Mecsektourist houses here now), with a colourful portal; and to the north of it a one-time Jesuit, later Cistercian monastery. Among the most famous buildings on Széchenyi tér is the **Hotel Nádor**, a luxury establishment with literary café, built in 1902. House **No 17**, almost on the corner, was once the residence of the Zsolnay family, whose eosin glazing and other ceramic creations played a vital role in the evolution of Hungarian art nouveau. And speaking of which, a few steps down Kossuth L u., which begins right there, you will find the **Hotel Palatinus**, a delightful example of art nouveau architecture.

The Fountain

Back on Széchenyi tér, turn left at the new town hall on the corner of Kossuth L u.. The little church that appears at the lower end of the square once belonged to the Capuchin order, and is now a part of the surgical clinic. The art nouveau **Fountain** in front of it, created as a memorial to Vilmos Zsolnay, was given to the town of Pécs by his son Miklós Zsolnay in 1930. The bulls' heads that form the spouts are made of pyrogranite and covered in eosin or crystalline glazing.

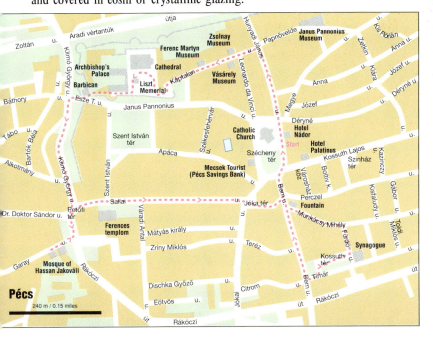

Amble down Munkácsy u., and left of the church take a right on Fürdő u. to reach Kossuth tér. The **Synagogue**, built in the 1860s, should be open. Bem u., on the other end of Kossuth tér, leads back to Széchenyi tér. Go up Szepessy Ignác u. until you reach **Káptalan u.**, Pécs's museum row. **No 2** houses two collections: one of the sculptor Amerigo (Imre) Tot (1909–84), who lived most of his life in Italy and favoured biblical motifs. The upstairs is entirely devoted to works from the Zsolnay factory, with table sets, vases, bowls with realistic depictions of snakes and leaves, tiles and even lamps.

The little house opposite was the birthplace of **Győző (Victor) Vásárely**, who made fame and fortune in Paris as a leading exponent of Op-Art. The rooms are devoted to his works on cloth and canvas and to works by his son and his apostles. A **Mining Museum** has been arranged in the cellar of the house, and extends underground all the way to Széchenyi tér. It has a superb collection of minerals right near the entrance. The next houses on Káptalan u. all have their museums exhibiting works by modern Hungarian artists. I would definitely recommend seeing the dramatic works – mostly graphics – of Ferenc Martyn (1899–1986) in **No 6**.

Modern art in Pécs

The street then takes you to a generous square with a large fountain, statues, a little café in a kind of gazebo, some Roman excavations and, most obvious of all, the Pécs **Cathedral**, whose four square towers wave over the city like mighty flags. Cathedrals have stood on this location since the beginning of Hungarian history, but this one was completed in 1891. The majestic interior was painted by several great Hungarian artists, notably Károly Lotz and Bertalan Székely whose *Coronation of András I* (near the southeastern tower) has become quite famous.

On leaving the cathedral, you will pass the **Bishop's Palace** on the right. A rather comical statue of Franz Liszt stands on the balcony. Turn right and head toward the old barbican of the medieval town wall. On the way you will encounter the statue of János Vitéz, the great Hungarian poet and humanist who lived from 1434 to 1472 and died in exile after conspiring against King Mátyás.

Take a left behind the barbican. You will soon see the **Mosque of Hassan Jakovali**, which has a full-fledged minaret, as well as a museum devoted to Turkish life in Hungary. Going back up to Petőfi tér and turning right, you will be on the Ferencsesek utcája, a

Forest near Pécs

pleasant pedestrian precinct that leads back to Széchenyi tér. The house with the elephant sign on one corner of Jokai tér used to belong to a trader in colonial goods.

It should be early afternoon by now, and after a bite at the restaurant of the **Palatinus Hotel**, it is time to leave Pécs for some outdoor activity. For children, there is the zoo situated on the well-marked road to Orfü to the northwest of town. Continue about 16km (10 miles) to the north, and you'll come to the artificial **Lakes of Orfü** in the Mecsek Hills, an excellent place for a swim If you are not into aquatic sports, visit the **Milling Museum** (Malom Müzeum) beside the lake, or drive on further to neighbouring **Abaliget** to inspect the cave, whose air is supposed to have a curative effect on lungs.

11. The Environs of Pécs

See minarets that were struck by lightning in Szigetvár, beautifully decorated local churches in the Ormánság, a castle with a dungeon museum in Siklós, and a wine museum in Villány.

Szigetvár, a little town of 13,000 inhabitants, lies 33km (20 miles) west of Pécs. Its name is known to every Hungarian for the valiant but futile resistance put up by Captain Miklós Zrínyi at the head of a tiny troup of defenders against the Turks in 1566. At the end they died heroes' deaths, and Zrínyi's grandson, a poet, recorded the tale in epic form. Suleiman II, 'the Great', died here in 1566 of causes unrelated to the war.

When arriving in town, stop at **Zrínyi tér**. On the southern side (to the left on entering the square) stands the first important Turkish relic: the **Mosque of Pasha Ali**. The ogee windows are original.

Women with a view

The minaret that once stood here was struck by lightning in 1715, and the rest of the mosque was zealously transformed into a Catholic church. The cupola, also surviving from the Turkish days, was decorated with a giant fresco by Dorfmeister.

A World War I memorial and a statue of Zrínyi also grace the square. Vár u., Castle Street, leads to the erstwhile fortified grounds. It might be too early to peek into the **Zrínyi Museum** on the left, but you can catch it on the way back. The castle consists of a fairly large, trapezoidal park surrounded by a wall. **Suleiman's Mosque** – he never enjoyed its earthly benefits – stands in its middle, flanked by a short minaret: coincidentally, lightning in the mid-18th century was responsible for amputating the upper two thirds. A castle museum has been ensconced here.

Leave Szigetvár in a westerly direction, and before the town boundary, go left in the direction of Hobol or Kétújfalu. After about 25km (16 miles) you will find a turning to the right (before Sellye) for **Drávaivány**. You are in the heart of the **Ormánság**, a rather special region known for a sociological curiosity: families were allowed only one child. Also, painter-carpenters decorated local churches with colourful coffered ceilings, and Drávaivány has one of the prettiest. **Vajszló**, on the way east toward Siklós, has a little museum with exhibits on the Ormánság. Further to the east is **Kovácshida**, where the local Protestant church has another coffered ceiling for inspection and a collection of Protestant art works.

Harkány is next, with a popular spa whose waters are beneficial for kinetic troubles. People with heart or circulatory problems should avoid it, however. **Siklós**, 5km (3 miles) to the east, is a fairly large town (it also has a spa) with a warm, bustling quality. Its main attraction, the **Castle**, stands on a small elevation in town and commands quite a view of the Dráva Valley. The earliest

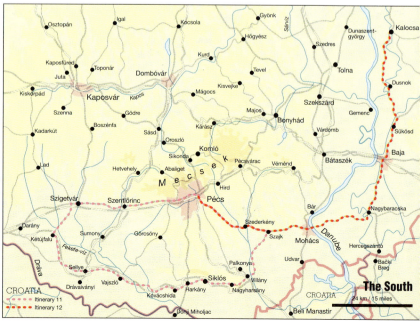

mention of the building was 1249, and it subsequently passed through some of Hungary's most eminent hands. The Garays had it, a family that produced several palatines, the son of King Mátyás owned it for a while, as did the Perényi dynasty. In spite of its apparent impregnability, the Turks captured it in a short battle in 1543. The Batthyány family held on to it almost uninterrupted from 1700 to 1873. Today it is in the public domain. Besides being the atmospheric site of a hotel, it also houses several museums, notably a Dungeon Museum, a Castle Museum (weapons, armour, etc), and some exhibitions of modern art and local pottery.

After lunch in the **Várpince Restaurant** at the foot of the castle, leave Siklós in an easterly direction (toward Villány). The landscape here is relatively arid, but it is excellent for growing wine. Stop briefly in the little church of **Nagyharsány**; its Gothic origins are still visible in a few frescos and a single stone column holding up the cupola. A short distance out of town, on the left-hand side, is the **Villány Sculpture Park**. The art exhibited here may not be to everyone's taste, but there are often very moving, interesting pieces.

Villány wine is famous

Villány, just up the road, is known for wine, and the **Wine Museum** is on the left shortly after entering town. It shows the tools of the trade, has wonderful collections of labels and special awards, and a cellar where the mould grows violently out of fresh pine barrels. Wine can be purchased and tasted at any number of places (drivers must remain teetotal!), but the best place is in one of the little cellars dug into the hillside with a little house at the entrance. A traditional wreath hanging over the door means the place is open.

This region of Hungary is virtually bilingual. The Danube Swabians who arrived here during the 18th century still speak German (and give their villages German names: Villány is Willand). If you do not decide to stay in Villány for a stroll and early dinner, you may visit the interior of the Swabian church in Palkonya which is on the way back to Pécs. The fact that it was once a mosque, however, will be quite obvious from its silhouette even at night.

To Mohács, the sight of Hungary's most famous defeat. An insight into life on the Danube, a look at the paprika industry and a visit to the prettiest train station in the country.

In memory of Mohács

Mohács, a town of nearly 22,000 inhabitants on the Danube, 40km (25 miles) east of Pécs (Route 57), stands at the top of the list of Hungary's great lost causes. At Mohács in 1526, Hungary lost its king along with his army, lost its unity and its independence. Thenceforth the nation was open to invasion by the Turks. No wonder that Hungarians console themselves when things are going badly by saying: 'It was worse at Mohács' (*Több is veszett Mohácsnál*).

The great battle took place south of town in the direction of Udvar, and for its 450th anniversary, the Hungarian government opened a memorial park with a forest of wooden statues representing the Turks, King Lajos II, the church dignitaries, and even the horses who died. It has a sombre atmosphere.

Mohács has long forgiven the Turks. The **Town Hall** on Széchenyi Square in the middle of town has a definitely Islamic look; the church there, built in 1926 for the 400th anniversary of the battle, is in Byzantine style. Coffee-houses and restaurants call themselves 'Turkish' (Török). Memories of the battle and of the days of Turkish occupation are to be found in the **Dorottya Kanizsai Museum** on Szerb u. to the north of town. (She was the wife of the palatine Perényi who died at Mohács, and legend has it she buried the dead there after the battle.) Next to the museum is a pretty Greek Orthodox **Church**, the third to be built on this site. Apart from the beautiful iconostasis, do not overlook the festival icons painted on wood. Two of them date from the late 1500s.

There are few bridges crossing the Danube in Hungary. Mohács has none, so you will have to cross using the ferry. Should this not be possible, drive north to Bátaszék and take Route 55 over to Baja. The road from the ferry leads to Baja through a very quiet landscape, with a handful of villages on the way.

The centre of **Baja** is Szentháromság tér (Trinity Square), an expansive plaza with a baroque Trinity column in the middle. The Sugovica, a tributary of the Danube, flows by the square's western side. It separates Baja from **Petőfi Island**, where there is a hotel, recreational opportunities and a few restaurants. Fish, of course, is a speciality here.

But either before or after lunch you should visit the **István Türr Museum** on the eastern side of the square where life on the Danube has been compressed into one superb exhibition, from stuffed fish and nets, to the bows of the *Anna*, a grain transporter. Several rooms are devoted to the traditional costumes and handiwork of local Slovaks, Germans and Hungarians. After leaving the museum take a right on Szentháromság tér, go down the pedestrian precinct and keep an eye out for the Táncsis Mihály u.. Here stands a large Greek Orthodox **Church**, with a particularly beautiful iconostasis.

The drive northward to **Kalocsa** along the alluvial plain of the Danube takes about 40 minutes. Kalocsa is an archbishopric going back to the days of István I himself, albeit the **Cathedral** is the fourth to be erected here and it is sheer baroque rather than Romanesque, having been designed by Andreas Mayerhoffer in 1735.

Ferry across the Danube

The painting over the main altar is by the great Austrian artist Leopold Kupelwieser. Next to the cathedral is the **Archbishop's Palace**, equally baroque. The great hall inside (Díszterem), where Franz Liszt gave many recitals, and the little chapel were decorated by Maulbertsch. Also visit the library, which boasts over 40,000 ancient volumes and codices, including a bible signed by Martin Luther.

About 70m (225ft) down István I u., to the left, is a small **museum** under the eaves of a new house, devoted to paprika, the local industry. Large black and white photographs bring back the past vividly, when it was still very much a cottage industry. There are displays of grinders, harvesting paraphernalia, paprika types and cans and packages of paprika and related goods. On leaving the museum, find your way to the train station (it lies at the end of Kossuth u. which also leads off from the cathedral square). The famous painter ladies (*pingaló asszonyok*) of Kalocsa have turned the station into one of the prettiest in Hungary, by covering everything in Kalocsai floral motifs.

On the way to or from the station look out for a sign indicating a museum, which will turn out to be a folk house painted in the same bright colours; no square metre was left untouched, neither the kitchen, the bargeboards, nor the bed; indeed, if the flowers were locusts they would be a plague. A shop here sells doilies, tablecloths and clothing embroidered in the same style, and next door is an agreeable café.

If you have dinner in Kalocsa (either the **Piros Arany**, meaning red gold, or the **Kalocsai Csárda**, both on István I u.) I suggest you plan your return trip to Pécs via Baja as the ferries over the Danube do not run all night.

Kalosca paprika

The Southeast

Famous words in stained glass

13. Szeged

Hungary's southern plain is in some ways the country's Garden of Eden. It has a lot of sun and water (the Tisza and Maros rivers), thermal waters, oil and paprika. The main centre is Szeged, 174km (108 miles) southeast of Budapest on the M5 motorway.

Szeged's great trauma – every Hungarian town has one – struck on 12 March 1879: the River Tisza broke its banks and destroyed the old town. Help immediately flooded in as well from towns throughout Europe, whose names were subsequently given to segments of the peripheral road. Kaiser Franz-Joseph II arrived and proclaimed, '*Szeged szebb lesz mint volt*,' or, 'Szeged will be more beautiful than it was.'

The famous words appear in the stained-glass window on the mezzanine of the **Town Hall**, a beautiful, yellow, neo-baroque building with a central tower, designed by Ödön Lechner and Gyula Partos in 1883. It stands on the western edge of the engaging **Széchenyi tér** which is barred to traffic and has jabbering fountains and stern statues under the thick frondage of old and rare trees. The Town Hall is connected to its neighbour in the south by a bridge of sighs.

Walk eastwards from the square along Wesselényi u., past the court and the theatre. To the left you will spot a statue of a violinist, the **Gypsy Pista Dankó**, and the building on his right is the **Deutsch Palace**, a typical Hungarian art nouveau construction. Szeged fortress used to stand here. Only one corner tower remains as a lookout platform over the river. The park that was laid out in its stead has been decorated with statues, notably of Queen Elizabeth, the wife of Franz-Joseph II. The palace-like building on the southern edge was built at the

Queen Elizabe

52

Art nouveau doorway

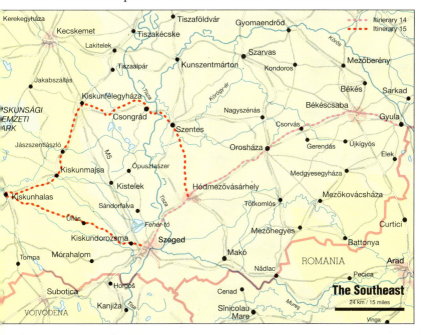

end of the 19th century and has always housed a museum (it has been called the **Ferenc Mora Museum** since 1950, after the 20th-century chronicler who lived in Szeged for many years). It has a number of separate exhibits that will take at least an hour and a half to get through, notably the iron and gold carvings, the gallery of Szeged's own artists, the Ferenc collection, peasant furniture and traditional costumes, and an exhibition of the trials and tribulations of the Kubikus, the day-labourers who did all the hard work straightening Hungarian rivers and building roads and dykes in pre-bulldozer days.

On leaving the museum wander down Oskola u. toward the cathedral. On the way turn into Somogyi u. to visit the romantic Fekete Ház, the **Black House**, one of the few buildings to have survived the flood. An exhibition of the Hungarian workers' movement continues to grace the upstairs chambers. Around the corner, by the way, is the **Hági Restaurant** where the atmosphere is lively and the food excellent, especially the famous spicy *Halászlé*, or fish soup.

The aforementioned **cathedral** is an unusual, large brick affair with two towers that appear almost disproportionately tall for the central section. The original architect was Frigyes Schulek, whose most famous work is the Mátyás Church in Budapest, but construction was not completed until 1930 because the old Demetrius

Church that stood here had to be torn down, causing much controversy. All that remains is the so-called **Demetrius Tower** standing watchfully on the cathedral square.

The interior is almost gaudy in its decoration, with not a square centimetre free of colourful ornamentation. There are depictions of the virtues, of saints, of Jesus, of the Holy Spirit, of the apostles. The centrepiece of the decoration is the **Szeged Madonna** over the main altar: she is in Hungarian-style folk costume and wearing typical red Szeged slippers.

A walk around the arcades of Szeged's **Medical University** should be included in a visit. The statues all represent the cream of Hungarian culture. The southern exit then leads to the Aradi vértanuk tér, a square often thronged by students, and to the right is Zrínyi u. followed by Jókai u. where a pedestrian precinct begins. Klauzal tere is where Kossuth, now in bronze effigy, made a rousing speech in October 1848. The **Virág Cukrászda** on the corner is the place to have some coffee and cake.

Kigyó u. leaves Klauzal tér in a westerly direction and becomes Hajnóczy u. beyond the ring road. The greyish building on the left, with a high-water marking carved in Hebrew and Hungarian, is the **Old Synagogue**. It has nothing in common with the new or **Great Synagogue** a few steps further. The entrance is on Jósika u.

This gigantic temple was designed in 1903 by Lipót Baumhorn, but the spiritual leader was Szeged's Rabbi Emmanuel Löw (1854–

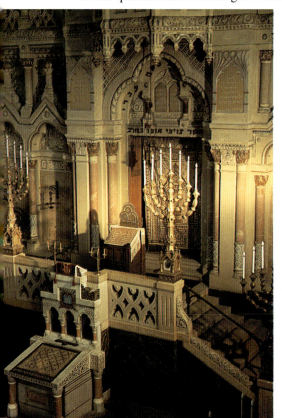

1944). The cupola is decorated on the inside in blue tiles with golden stars. The stained-glass windows are painted representations of flowers which were taken from Löw's book entitled *The Flora of the Jews*.

Gogol u. takes you back to the town centre. The rest of the day can be spent either luxuriating at the **Steam Bath** on Kálvin tér, or visiting the **National Historic Park** in Opusztaszer, 30km (18 miles) to the north, where, according to Hungarian mythology, the seven Magyar tribes assembled while they were extending their control over the Carpathian Basin.

Inside the Old Synagogue

14. Across the Great Plain

The art of the Great Plain and a monument to potters in Hód-mezővásárhely, followed either by a mud bath in Orosháza or some spicy sausage in Békéscsaba. After a visit to the fortress in Gyula, complete the afternoon with coffee and cake at a 100-year-old patisserie.

Hódmezővásárhely lies 25km (16 miles) northeast of Szeged on Route 47. Its main claim to fame is majolica and porcelain, much of which is now exported. The town hall tower is visible from a distance, and it watches over the shady **Kossuth tér** (parking available in side streets). In the centre stands a **Hussar Memorial**. Standing on the town hall steps, it looks as if the rider's sword were aimed at the little Mercury topping the dome of the art nouveau building opposite (the Hungarian National Bank). The building

In memory of war

to the right of the town hall now houses the **Alföldi Galéria**, the Gallery of the Great Plain, with a very fine exhibition of the works of a number of painters who took their inspiration from the nature and people of the region. The most important of them, perhaps, is local man János Tornyai (1869–1936). Here you will find his moving *Bús magyar sors*, or 'Sad Hungarian Fate', a lonely horse on a deserted field, and in the dramatic *Vihar*, or 'Storm'.

The Great Plain

Walk up Szántó Kovács János u. to the baroque Greek Orthodox church. Across the street is the **János Tornyai Museum** which has an important prehistoric collection. Back on the level of Kossuth tér stands the old **Protestant Church**, which dates to the beginning of the 18th century. Its brightly painted organ loft was unfortunately carted off to Budapest to be exhibited in the Museum of Applied Arts. Take a left here, and you will soon come to the Catholic church and a column of pyrogranite standing before it. This is a monument to the potters of Hódmezővásárhely. Bajcsy-Zsilinszky u., right after the church, takes you to the **Porcelain Manufacture**, which is open during business hours.

On the way out of Hódmezővásárhely on Route 47 keep an eye out on the right for the **Synagogue**, a spectacular white, art nouveau building that has just been restored and serves as a cultural centre. After that, continue on to Békéscsaba. On the way is **Orosháza**, which boasts a little **Museum** of local history and culture named after János Szántó Kovács, a local man who was involved mainly in agrarian politics. Orosháza also attracts crowds

The fortress at Gyula, unusually constructed from brick

of enthusiasts to its mud bath and spa about 5km (3 miles) on the way to Szentes. If you choose this, it'll take the whole afternoon.

Otherwise, continue down Route 47 to **Békéscsaba**, the capital of Békés county, famous throughout Hungary and even beyond for its spicy **Csabai sausage**. Eating here might not be a bad idea if you feel hungry: try the **Fehér Galamb** in Kazinczy u.. This part of the country was settled by Slovaks and Germans, and the museum on Széchenyi u. around the corner from the Csaba Hotel displays their costumes and items from their everyday lives. Across the road is a gallery devoted to one of Hungary's most famous painters, Mihály Munkácsy (1844–1900), a romantic who lived and learned in Paris. Just outside Békéscsaba, on the way to Gyula, visit the **Grain Museum**. It has a traditional farmhouse, a windmill and samples of 24 different types of grain on display.

The rest of the day (from about 2pm onward) should be spent in **Gyula**, an attractive town on the Romanian border. Albert Dürer, the father of the great German painter Albrecht Dürer, was born here, as was Ferenc Erkel, the 19th-century composer who not only provided the music to the national anthem, but also wrote Hungary's first 'national' opera, *Bán Bánk*.

Begin at Gyula's **Fortress**, an unusual construction made of brick, with a modern equestrian statue (by Béla Tóth) in front. An outer ring of fortifications was once built as an additional — and ultimately useless — measure against the Turks, but it no longer exists. Today the little yard is used for theatrical performances, and within the walls is a little museum. The path leading straight away from the castle's entrance takes you to the **Castle Baths**, a wonderful neoclassical building. Next to it is a pretty Greek Catholic church with a fine iconostasis. The door is usually open, though a gate prevents entrance into the church itself.

Home with the vegetables

The real centre of town is **Petőfi tér** (about 8 minutes on foot down Kossuth L u.). Particularly majestic is the **Town Hall** on the right, with its ornate tower and an 18th-century church opposite. Around the left-hand side is the **100-year-old patisserie** (Szazéves Cukrászda). While waiting for coffee and cake have a look at the pastry-cook exhibition in the back room of the shop.

15. The Kiskunság

A drive through Little Cumania, starting at the Lace Museum in Kiskunhalas and finishing up at the delightful Halászfalu (fisher village) at Csongrád.

The name 'kun' in Hungary appears frequently as an element of a larger name, and generally only in a specific area. It refers to territories granted by King Béla IV to the heathen Cumanian tribesmen in the 13th century, in return for help in the defence against the Mongols. The sandy soil of the **Kiskunság** (Little Cumania) has endowed the region with very fine wines. And if the sun gets too unbearable, my advice is to cool off in any of the spas or lakes.

Kiskunhalas is about 57km (36 miles) from Szeged on a straight and narrow road. Once here, take a left at the first large intersection (there is a supermarket on your right). The little house with arched windows in the middle of a small park is the most important **Museum** in town, for it gives a concentrated look at what made Kiskunhalas famous, namely lace. It all started at the beginning of the 20th century, when the seamstress Mária Markovits started making lace to the designs of a drawing teacher named Árpád Dékány. After success at the World Fair in St Louis in 1904, they never looked back. Mária Markovits is immortalised in bronze in front of the museum. Another handicraft performed in Kiskunhalas, albeit on a much more modest scale, is saddlemaking: Mr Abonyi shows his skills in his atelier on Vass u. 1 (ask for directions).

The next goal is the real centre of town, **Hősök tere**, a shady place with a cross-section of Hungarian architectural styles. The **Protestant Church** has a baroque exterior that belies the simplicity of its interior. Next to it is the neoclassical **Town Hall**, dating from 1834. Opposite is an art nouveau complex with a striking tower. This is also where you will find the **Thorma János Museum**, with exhibits from the city's past.

Opposite the Town Hall

The next stop is **Kiskunmajsa**, 25km (16 miles) to the northeast, whose only real claim to fame is its spa on the outside of town. For lunch, the restaurant on the grounds of the spa is cheap and good in a homey way.

Kiskunfélegyháza is a pleasant, provincial town of about 36,000 people. If you come in on Kossuth u., you will see the neo-Renaissance **Szent István**

Church on your left. Its architect was Gyula Partos, who helped Lechner on Kecskemét's town Hall (*see Itinerary 5*). Kiskunfélegy-háza's own **Town Hall** is a striking art nouveau building heavily decorated with typically Hungarian motifs, hearts and flowers, made of Zsolnay majolica. Diag-onally opposite is the **Hattyúház** (Swan House), built in 1820 by János Mayer-hoffer, and named for a swan portrayed on its facade. Finally, to the north on the main road, you will find the **Kiskun Museum** (on the right). The windmill in the yard is an authentic relic from the days when the area was known for its flour. The museum displays regional folkloric and social ephemera, and the prison that used to be here has also become a museum. Its most eminent inmate was Sándor Rozsa, a leader of the Betyárs, a band of often shady characters with some similarity to Robin Hood's Merry Men.

Another half-hour to the east on Route 451 is **Csongrád**, whose obviously Slav name refers to a 'Black Castle'. It no longer exists. The local museum on Széchenyi út (on the way in) does tell something about the past of the town. A little further on you will encounter Kos-suth tér, whose most prominent feature is the art nouveau school building in the middle of the fork in the road. Bypass it on the left and stop in at the **Kubikus Museum** (Kubikus were the labourers who straightened rivers and built roads). These poor fellows had a particularly hard time around Csongrád which, as the map re-veals, sits on the confluence of the Körös and Tisza rivers.

The Town Hall, Kiskunfélegyháza

Csongrád has a second town centre, in fact a particularly beautiful one with rows of whitewashed houses snuggled under thatched roofs. It is to the left on leaving the museum, and should be driven to if time is becoming short (it should be about 4pm by now). One of the little thatched houses has been turned into a museum (local peasant life) and several are for rent for holiday-makers, something to keep in mind for the future. The **Halászfalu** (fisher village), as it is known, also has a few nice restaurants with fish specialities. An alternative for the evening is to proceed back to Szeged via **Szentes** (several art nouveau buildings) and have a dinner there (**Fekete Bárány étterem** or the **Petőfi étterem**, for example).

16. Debrecen

Debrecen was long known as 'the Calvinist Rome' because of its importance to the Protestants of east central Europe. A tour of the main sights is followed by an afternoon excursion on to the steppe of the Hortobágy Puszta.

The region east of the Tisza, so-called Tiszántúl in Hungarian, is eastern Hungary per se, and the local capital, situated 233km (145 miles) east of Budapest, is Debrecen. In fact, Debrecen, dusty, weary, wearing its communist housing relics like a crown of thorns, could be considered Hungary's second or alternative capital. Several times in the past it served this purpose. It has had a difficult history, though its role as a market centre has always helped it along rather well. It could well afford to pay tribute during the Turkish occupation, meaning it was spared some of the damage inflicted on other towns, but its Protestantism made the Habsburgs particularly wrath-

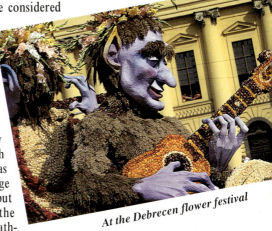

At the Debrecen flower festival

ful. Also, having only an underground water supply under the Great Forest (Nagyerdő) meant that whenever something caught fire the whole town burned down. This explains the phoenix in Debrecen's coat-of-arms.

Most visitors to Debrecen come for the **Hortobágy Puszta** at the town's door, that special section of the Great Plain where there is no horizon and, if we are to believe the brochures, fellows with bushy moustaches and dressed in traditional garb ride across the landscape. They do, but for the most part for show rather than any traditional purpose. The other reason to come is the **Flower Festival** which takes place on 20 August.

But Debrecen on its own has a few charms. Begin the day with

The Nagytemplon

an early-morning coffee at the **Arany Bika**, the oldest and certainly most beautiful hotel in town. The current building is the creation of the architect Hajós who incidentally won gold at the 100m and 1200m swimming heats at the 1896 Olympics, the first of the Modern Games.

The Bika is within sight of the **Nagytemplom**, the great church, which, like Debrecen itself, burned down and was rebuilt several times. The current building dates from 1805–27, and it is in sober, classical style. The interior has all the dignity and simplicity one expects of a Calvinist temple, with plain white walls and hard, dark wooden pews. The armchair next to the altar was used by Kossuth himself at this very location to read the declaration of independence from the Habsburgs on 14 April 1849.

Before entering the Nagytemplom, go in the opposite direction on Nagytemplom u., and visit the **Kistemplom**, the Little Church, whose tower hardly looks as if it belongs to a church. It was built in baroque style, but renovated in the 1870s and given a new look.

After visiting the Nagytemplom, go to the back to the little **Mémorial Park**. The statue here recalls the Protestant pastors who were sent to pull an oar by the Catholic Habsburgs in 1675. They were liberated by the Dutch Captain Ruyter a year later.

Behind the park is the **Protestant College** (*orando et laborando* stands above the door), which is still active. There is a small

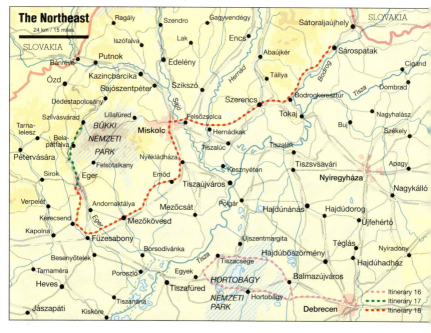

museum which details life in the college in the old days. It displays some of the practical experiments in physics, a Siemens-Halske generator, the Magdeburg Vacuum Ball, steam engines and pumps. There is also a meteorite that landed nearby in 1857.

Leaving the college, take a right until you reach a symmetrical building with a typically Empire-style colonnade at the entrance. This is the **Déri Museum**, housing the wonderfully eclectic collections of Frigyes Déri, a wealthy silk manufacturer. They include ancient Egyptian art, art from the 15th to the 19th century, especially paintings by Munkácsy and Bertalan Székely, traditional pottery, faïence, glass work and furniture.

Before heading out to Hortobágy, stop at the **tourist office** across the street from the Nagytemplom (to its right), and find out about the Puszta, where you'll be able to see original Hungarian cattle ranging freely and watch the stunning displays of the *csikós*, the Hungarian horse-herders. On the way out to Hortobágy, watch for a little house on the right with a cart or two out front: a woman potter works here specialising in black pottery, which is achieved by placing the pottery in a smoky, coal-fired kiln.

Hortobágy itself, 38km (24 miles) west of Debrecen, is hardly a village at all, but rather an accumulation of houses located on the road that has been used since the Middle Ages as a trade route to Western Europe. The *csárda* (restaurant) here is rather good. It is also – like all *csárdas* along this road – in a traditional horse-changing inn. The **nine-arch bridge** (Kilenlyukú híd) crossing the Hortobágy River was completed in 1833, replacing a somewhat shakier wooden construction. Opposite the *csárda* is the **Hortobágy Gallery** with artistic representations of the Puszta by Munkácsy, Ferenc Medgyessy, Mór Thán and János Pásztor. Across the road is a **museum** with displays of life on the range.

Playing in Hortobágy

Among the finest exhibits are the handicrafts of the men who watched the animals, who whiled away long hours out in the open carving sticks and tobacco boxes and embroidering their clothing, especially their great woollen coats. In front of the museum stands the *Shepherd* by Árpád Somogyi, and a little further on is his *People of the Great Plain*.

Every year the 19th and 20th of August are wild days out in Hortobágy, with huge celebrations for the feast of St István. The traditional bridge market (*Hídivásár*) has been attracting ever-larger crowds of merchants, peddling anything from watermelon to antique clothing. Older Hungarians in costume sometimes play music near the drink stands. An afternoon

A poetic landscape

drive through this poetic landscape should not be aimless. Drive west until the turn-off for Egyek, and head to **Tiszacsege**. You are virtually in the heart of Hungary. The restaurant by Csege beach is a ramshackle construction lit by fluorescent tubes and ringing with drinking songs. The food is excellent.

17. Eger

Europe's northernmost Turkish minaret stands proudly on a little square in Hungary's prettiest town, Eger. It lies in a valley between the Mátra and Bükk ranges, some 140km (87 miles) east of Budapest. The region is known for its wine, particularly Egri Bikavér, Eger Bull's Blood, a mixture of several red wines, aromatic, fruity and strong.

Eger was István I's first bishopric. The **Fortress** that still stands over the town was built after the Mongol invasion of 1271. As the Turkish threat grew after Mohács, Tamás Varkoch and later István

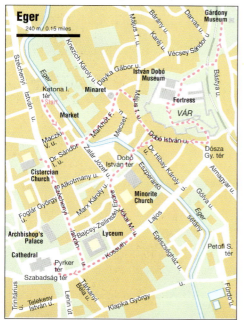

Dobó worked hard to prepare for an assault. It began on 11 September 1552 and ended a month later with a Hungarian victory. Dobó was celebrated as a hero throughout the land, and so were the women of Eger who participated in pouring boiling oil on the infidel. Forty-four years later the Turks resumed their attack and took the city. After the return of Habsburg rule, much of the fortress was destroyed to prevent it being used by Hungarian rebels.

Begin with breakfast at the market held in a modern building on **István Katona tér**. A gentle walk takes you to the minaret, whose mosque was torn down in 1841. Proceed then through the tortuous streets that lead to Dobó u. and then up to the fortress. Standing on the **Dobó Bastion** (left of the ticket booth), you have a spectacular view over the town. The casemates can be visited but only on a guided tour, which can take time. The dungeons are also open to the public, with an exhibition of the tools of the hangman's trade.

The former Bishop's Palace, with its attractive Gothic arcade, stands at the northern end of the interior courtyard, where you will also find a 64m (210ft) well and the picture gallery. The building now houses the **István Dobó Museum**, whose Heroes' Hall on the ground floor displays memorabilia recalling the defence of Eger. Upstairs are items relating to the history of the fortress: stones, clothing, weapons, chalices and diverse ephemera. The tower next to the palace houses a mint which still produces memorial medals. After strolling around the ruins, leave via the northern gate. This leads to the little house where Géza Gárdony lived from 1897 until his death in 1922. He wrote *The Stars of Eger*, a popular historical novel.

Go back through the fortress and down to **Dobó tér**, the traditional marketplace. The two statues here, one of Dobó himself, the

Europe's northernmost Turkish minaret

other called *The Battles of the Border Forts* and depicting Turks, Hungarians and three horses in a lethal clinch, are both by Zsigmond Kisfaludi Strobl. The **Minorite Church** (1758–73) is the dominant feature on the square, a splendid, baroque edifice in apricot pink. The Austrian artist Johann Lukas Kracker was responsible for the painting over the altar of this three-aisled church. Next to it is an ancient pharmacy.

Follow Jokai M u. to Kossuth L u., and and turn left to see the two wrought-iron gates by the Würzburg artist Henrik Fazola in the County Hall. Then head in the other direction on Kossuth u..

Cistercian church near Bélapátfalva

The great building on the right is the **Lyceum**, a school erected by the enlightened dignitaries of Eger between 1763 and 1785. It was supposed to be a university, but the Habsburg Emperor Joseph II did not permit it. It has an observatory (now a museum) and a library with over 100,000 volumes and a magnificent ceiling fresco painted by Kracker depicting the Council of Trent. Another neck-wrenching visit is to the chapel next to the library: Franz Anton Maulbertsch created this light, airy, almost transparent depiction of the divine heavens.

Across the street from the Lyceum is the **Cathedral**. It was born a church, became a mosque, was rebuilt by Giovanni Battista Carlone in baroque style (1715–27) and finally revamped by József Hild in neoclassical style (1831–37). The great stairs leading to the portico are flanked by statues of István I and László I, Hungary's two canonised kings. The ceiling inside was painted in a subdued modern style by István Takács. (A tip: avoid the restaurant below the cathedral. Those around Dobó tér are better.) On leaving the cathedral take Széchenyi u. left. It leads past the baroque-style **Archbishop's Palace**, and to the Cistercian church.

The rest of the day should be spent on a short drive northward. The first stop is in, or rather near, **Bélapátfalva** (15km/9 miles) for a visit to the former Cistercian church and monastery, the latter only a stone pattern on the floor. The church, originally built in 1232, was rebuilt in the 15th and 18th centuries.

Eight kilometres (5 miles) further comes **Szilvásvárad**, which is a breeding place for the famous Lipizzàner horse. The museum devoted to this breed is in the middle of the village on the right. There is a stable, too; check the local tourist office for shows. Finally, if you can stand one more museum, the **Orbán House** (past the Lipizzaner museum on the left), a pretty farmhouse with a portico, documents the local natural history. Another way of experiencing the same is a walk up the valley of the Szalajka. The path is enlivened with displays of the hard life of the forest workers.

Plan for a dinner in Eger. Begin by a visit to the **Wine Museum** at Városfal u.1. It is open until 10pm and offers wine tasting. Then take a taxi to the **Szépasszonyok völgye** (Valley of the Fair Maidens) where the Eger wine-makers have their cliff cellars. Tasting, buying and dinner can all be enjoyed here.

Hungarian embroidery in Mezőkövesd followed by a tour of the churches in Miskolc. Then east to admire the castle in Sárospatak.

From Eger, there are two ways of getting to Miskolc. The first is the scenic route over the Bükk Mountains, along the winding mountain road that begins in **Felsőtárkány**. It leads past small settlements of charcoal burners, and through **Lillafüred**, where you will find a cavern (*Szt István barlang*), a smelting museum and the Palota Hotel. Over to the right just before Miskolc you will see the four square towers of **Diosgyőr Castle**. Built in the 13th century, it had a glorious period in the 14th and 15th centuries, deteriorated when it was a fortress on the border of Europe during the Ottoman era, and finally was emasculated by the Habsburgs to prevent it being used by Hungarians. It has a museum and also provides the dramatic setting for theatrical productions in summer.

As an avid fan of Hungarian folklore, however, I would be more inclined to drive to Miskolc by the second route via **Mezőkövesd**, a small town 18km (11 miles) south of Eger on Route 3. It was granted rights by King Mátyás in the 15th century and the local people have been known as the Matyó ever since. Their fame in Hungary rests on the rich embroidery with which they embellish their long skirts, aprons, blouses and shirts. Regional history and folk art is explored in the **Matyó Museum** in the House of Culture on the main square, as well as the **Matyó Ház** on Béke tér 2.

Local embroidery

Hungary's third-largest city, **Miskolc**, is best known for its noisy and polluting steelworks. But the inner city has been nicely restored and contains interesting churches, as well as fine baroque houses. Once you've arrived, find Hősök tere, the main square. The **Minorite Church** standing on the northern side was built by Giovanni Battista Carlone between 1729 and 1734. About 45m (150ft) behind it, wrapped in the greenery of a small park, is a **Greek Orthodox Church** with a fine iconostasis by Miklós Jankovics. The history and culture of the Orthodox Church in general is exhibited in the neighbouring museum.

Walk past the **Miskolc synagogue** while heading south to the **Avas Hill**.

Miskolc has more than meets the eye

Then take a right on Széchenyi u. and a left a little further on: the shingle-covered steeple of the Avas church's **bell-tower** should serve as a beacon. The tower was built in 1685 (the older version burned down). It stands in the midst of an ancient cemetery, allegedly in use since the 11th century. The harmonious three-aisled church, of Calvinist creed, was built in the mid-16th century. It has a simple coffered ceiling, the walls are white except for a few 18th-century paintings and decorative items from eastern Hungary's church history. Its *pièce de résistance* is a Renaissance choir stall. At the foot of the hill is another, recently restored and obviously Gothic building that once functioned as a Protestant college. Nowadays it provides space for the **Ottó Herman Museum**, named after a renowned Hungarian ethnographer and anthropologist.

Have lunch in Miskolc before heading east along Route 37 to **Sárospatak**, 84km (52 miles) away. Take the first exit in order to drive past the House of Culture, an unmistakably modern construction by Imre Makovec. At the main road go right and then left two streets after passing the Bodrog Hotel. The statue of St Elisabeth and her son Lajos in front of the Catholic church is by Imre Várga, one of Hungary's most distinguished sculptors. Further on you come to the castle: on the right before the entrance is the Borostyán Hotel in a former Dominican cloister and church.

The **Castle** was built during the Renaissance period by the Perényi dynasty and ultimately became a Rákóczi possession. The

Resting the legs

oldest surviving section is the Red Tower, which used to stand in the middle and is now in the southeastern corner. The oriel in the northeastern corner of the palace is perhaps the most significant room, for it was here that Ferenc Rákóczi I swore an ill-fated oath against the Habsburgs in 1670.

There are a number of interesting exhibitions and museums in the castle's rooms, from historic documents to implements of the wine trade. Afterwards, drive back to Sárospatak's main street, take the first left for a brief look at the new school, another Makovec creation, then turn around and find the **Protestant College**, which has two important collections: a library and a museum of student life. This simple college has an impressive list of former pupils: Kossuth, Kazinczy (the 'reformer of the Hungarian language'), and Mihály Csokonai Vitéz, poet and playwright.

On the way back to Eger stop off at **Tokaj**, which has a museum with an emphasis on the local product: wine, the 'king of wines and the wine of kings', as the saying goes, but you may have seen enough for the day. The local tourist office could direct you to a wine-tasting where you can learn all about the grading of Tokaj wines. Only the driver need abstain.

Sunflowers are everywhere

Shopping

When it comes to shopping, Hungary is a consumer's paradise both for the Austrians, who swamp the western towns for inexpensive food from carrots to cakes, and for the Romanians and Ukrainians who crawl along the roads in overfilled vehicles on the look-out for any food at all. The latter have also started filling up the flea-markets and standing around main squares selling wares from the attic, which can be a boon for the traveller in search of a bargain in embroidered cloths, old crockery and household tools, military paraphernalia, communist insignia and even old books. Be a little careful, though: cloth that looks old but feels like the by-product of the petrol industry is more than often fake. Hand-painted plates are not all old, either, though if they are pretty they might just be worth the price.

Markets

Shopping in Hungarian markets can be great fun. The bustle recalls the good old days of small-town mercantilism when everyone from the big farmer to the humble widowed peasant woman sold their produce directly. They bring live chickens, geese and rabbits, and with them comes a motley crowd of gypsies and other privateers who also have something to peddle: normally honey, wine, wooden bowls, home-made toothpaste, moonshine or knitwear. The sausage-

Spoilt for choice

mongers come out in force to provide sustenance to the buyers.

The markets remain a social event and are therefore a kind of human museum for the visitor. Every major town has its market hall (*vásárcsarnok*), and larger department stores are usually nearby. If you are in Hungary with your own car, consider the purchase of some Hungarian fruit and vegetables, some salami (which is not as cheap as one might think), hot *csabai* sausage, honey and seeds.

Wines and spirits, while not directly sold at markets, are also widely available. A few bottles of *Tokaj aszú*, the sherry-like wine made of late-harvested grapes soaked in wine, and some *Egri bikaver* (Eger bull's blood) belong on the standard shopping-list. But as these are readily available in the West, you may want to take home your favourite from a wine-tasting in Eger, Tokaj, Villány or from the Kiskun region. Keep the customs limits in mind (see *Practical Information*).

Then there are the flea-markets (*bolhapiac*), such as the one on the Nagykörösi út in Budapest (on the way to Kecskemét). It tends to be expensive and bargaining, which is the fun of flea-markets, is hard. But every now and then you can still find a great buy. Out in the country most flea-markets are general, open markets that include sellers of new goods, often from Romanian, Ukrainian, Polish, Serbian or Slovak department stores. There are, of course, the real flea-marketeers mentioned above and the professional junk-dealers, many of whom have stores somewhere in Hungary. Also usually present arc a fine crowd of basket-weavers, brush-makers, woodcarvers, whip-makers, tanners, glass-blowers, metalworkers, silversmiths and other craftspeople. There are also innumerable peddlers of easily identifiable industrial folklore, usually in the form of

Floral design

chess sets with pieces no player could properly play with, lathed pens, walking sticks, and the like. The most egregious figures are the textile dealers with across-the-board cheap and hideous clothing, and the dealers in cassette tapes assaulting passers-by with a broadside of stylised Hungarian folk music. Pécs and Szeged are known for their markets, and the Hídivásár in Hortobágy on 19 and 20 August is an important consumer venue.

Handicrafts

Flowery designs, intricate ornamentation, and liberal and bold use of bright colours make Hungarian folk art noticeable and quite attractive. Many items are available for purchase often at reasonable prices in markets and shops, even in museums. Sometimes, however, the folklore is so stylised as to enter the realm of pure kitsch. The best way to get a feel for the 'genuine' style is to visit the regional museums, which often exhibit handicrafts.

Specific towns and areas are known for specific items or styles. In Kalocsa and Mezőkövesd the designs are mainly floral (with hearts), and come in any form, embroidery, pottery, or clothing. Even local furniture is painted. Kiskunhalas is famous for its lace. Palozan handicrafts, embroidery and pottery are available in Hollókő and in the Palozan cooperative in Szécsény. Mohács has black pottery, whose glazing comes from the soot of a smoky, coal-fired kiln. Hódmezővásárhely is also famous for its pottery, which has simple, generally abstract designs on it. Pottery, by the way, is an important activity in Hungary. Wherever you see a sign pointing to a *Fázékás*, go and have

Black pottery at Hortóbagy

a look. You will find vases, plates, cups, mugs, jugs, candleholders and more. In addition, you will be supporting a local artist. (Other potter towns are Magyarszombatfa to the west of the Danube and, in the east, Pásztó, Gyöngyös, Kalocsa, Mezőtúr, Nádud-vár, Hajduszoboszló and Sarospatak.) Burning designs in leather or embroidering leather vests is quite a widespread activity. Blue print is a speciality around Pécs.

Specialised shops in the centre of Budapest (along Váci u., for example) and in larger department stores also offer handicrafts.

Hungary has three famous porcelain factories. The most important is in Herend, north of Lake Balaton. It has been in operation since 1839. Before buying, visit the porcelain museum. Zsolnay porcelain from Pécs is also interesting. Finally, there is the tiny community of Hollóháza in the mountains north of Sarospatak. Once again, you should examine the exhibition first to gain a sense of the true style.

Antiques

The words *régiség* and *ántikvitás* indicate an antique dealer, and the same caveats apply as in the West. Prices in Budapest and along the tourist routes are often quite inflated. Folkloric items, just because they are in a shop and not on a peddler's carpet, are not necessarily authentic, though the price in hard currency is. Used books and musical manuscripts are by and large a good buy. Budapest has a number of used book stores, on the Váci u., on Múzeum körút and near Deák tér on Andrássy út.

And finally, Hungarians still repair almost anything, from old typewriters to shoes, providing a service that is rapidly dying out in Western Europe. You may have the odd item in your cellar or attic that could use an overhaul.

Eating Out

Just as they threw themselves at vastly superior armies of Mongols and Turks, the Magyars daily defy a *force majeure* of cholesterols and other nutritional enemies with bold knife and fork. The reason is obvious at first bite: Hungarian food, when well prepared, is a sin the Catholic Church has not yet put on the index. It is tasty, spicy, warming, filling, but does take a little time to get used to for unacclimatised stomachs. The bottom of every pot, pan or baking tray is inevitably greased with pork fat, which brings out flavours; onions and garlic are generously used; and meat, particularly pork, is a staple, which makes life for vegetarians a little difficult. Paprika – which gives most Hungarian dishes their tang – is liberally deployed.

The Menu

Tourist business means that restaurateurs often provide menus in various languages (normally German precedes English), but translations can be unreliable. *Levesek* means soups, which for the average mortal is a light liquid introducing a meal. Broths, such as the *Ujházi* chicken soup (*tyukleves*), or vegetable cream soups serve the purpose well. A Hungarian speciality is *gyümölcsleves*, or fruit

soup. This strange concoction sometimes comes with a topping of whipped cream (*habbal*). Two soups deserve special care, as they are very filling: *Jokai bableves*, a bean soup with sausage and a slab of smoked pork named after the poet Mór Jokai, who came up with the idea; and *Bográcsgulyás*, a soupy goulash, which you will be served if you simply ask for 'goulash'. *Előételek*, appetisers, come in warm (*meleg*) or cold (*hideg*).

The *Hortobágyi palacsinta* is found here, a pancake with a meat filling, usually *pörkölt* (*see page 72*). The

Adding local flavour

famous *lecso* is a stew of smoked bacon, sausage, peppers, paprika, onions and tomatoes.

Ajánlatok means 'specialities' and if you are near a major stretch of water will often include fish. Szeged is famous for fisherman's soup (*halászlé*), which you can find all along the Tisza and even the Danube. It is quite sharp and should include a little bit of roe (*ikra*). The Balaton produces the pike-perch named *fogas*, but the dwindling supply has caused prices to rise quite high.

Of course, no trip to Hungary will be complete without goulash, a derivation of the word *gulyás*, which refers to the Hungarian cow-punchers. That reddish stew based on onions, pork fat and paprika is called either *pörkölt*, *paprikás* or *tokány* in Hungarian, with minor differences in taste between them. Goulash is best eaten with *galuska*, dumplings, or *tarhonya*, pellets of wheat dough. *Székely gulyás* is a soupy *pörkölt* with sauerkraut and a portion of sour cream on top.

Other common dishes are the *pecsenye*, or roasts, *Cigány pecsenye* being fried slabs of pork, bacon and a Frankfurter; *Brassói pecsenye* is chopped ham and potatoes. Foods described as *rantott* are fried in batter. Hocks, *csülök*, are another Hungarian speciality.

The accompaniment to these dishes, if not specifically mentioned already, can be found under *körételek* and includes rice, greens, usually peas or green beans, potatoes in the form of French fries, home fries, croquettes and sometimes mashed. *Saláták* is for the most part pickled vegetables, tomatoes or cucumber. As for dessert, it comes under the menu-heading *tészták*, meaning pastries. *Palacsinta*, the thin Hungarian pancake filled with jam, farmer's cheese or chocolate is a must. *Gundel palacsinta* is filled with nuts and a heavy chocolate sauce. *Rétes*, strudel, is always tasty when fresh. *Turos csusza töpörtyüvel*, strangely enough, is not a dessert but a meal of noodles with farmer's cheese and cracklings.

Drink

All varieties of wine are available. The great wine areas are south of Pécs, on the northern shore of Lake Balaton, the sandy earth around Kiskunhalas, Eger and Tokaj. Even Budapest has some vineyards. Czech beers are frequently available.

Sample Kőbányai beer from the outskirts of Pest to quench a thirst. The town of Nagykanizsa also has a good brewery. Otherwise, Hungary has a great deal of excellent fruit juices, which, if sold in more attractive bottles, could be an international hit. Unicum, in the round bottle, combats heavy meals: it is so horribly bitter, that only the stomach that needs it can take it.

Restaurants

Hungary has, by and large, no dearth of restaurants. They run under several names (*vendéglő*, *csárda*, *étterem*), none of which divulges the actual quality of the food. Even allegedly better hotel restaurants sometimes provide meals several degrees below canteen level.

The *csárdás*, always a draw for tourists looking for the elusive mustachioed Hungarian *ranchero*, are often located in traditional whitewashed houses with thatched roofs and mellifluous porticos. My experience has often been good in these places.

The menus outside the restaurants reveal the class (*osztály* or simply *oszt.*), with first-class being high-priced to expensive, and third-class being inexpensive to cheap. Some tips are: if a third-class smoky cavern is full of eating – and talking – Hungarians, the chances are it is excellent and homey. The same applies to the second-class places, though ventilation and decoration will generally be better. First-class and luxury venues are less crowded, and the menus often less typically Hungarian, which[1] in the case of greens and salads can be a blessing.

Among the most frequently encountered problems are obnoxious waiters, especially in the touristically popular areas. Lukewarm cooking is also a speciality that has to be countered with friendly firmness. The microwave is a culinary Fifth Column in Hungarian restaurants that tends to make fluffy *galuska* taste like pebbles and turns *palacsinta* into a coat of mail. Music always accompanies the meal, be it by a gypsy band, a local crooner on a Hammond organ, or through loudspeakers discreetly sunken into the ceilings. Sometimes the music is fun, sometimes merely loud.

Since the late 1980s there has been a move toward healthier eating, with clean, light surroundings and the odd vegetarian dish on the menu. Furthermore, the ubiquitous fast food has ploughed its way into the country. But Hungarians make hamburgers, too, albeit of pork. *Virsli* is a sausage (from the German *Wurst*); and *hurka* is a sausage stuffed with a spicy mixture of meat and rice; *lángos*, fried dough that can be garnished with cheese, onions or sour cream, is another popular item at stands by the side of the road or at the spas. Lately salad bars have started popping up. Their fare is usually heavy, creamy, mayonnaise-drowned (plain lettuce, carrots and the like still elude the traveller), but tasty. Magyarised pizza is another dish to try. As for snacks, everyone offers *pogácsa*, a bun of shortened dough. And if you tire of Hungarian food, pizzerias are everywhere.

Another option is to picnic: the land, especially in summer, is bountiful, with excellent fruit and vegetables, apples, peaches, apricots, plums, grapes, tomatoes, celery, carrots and more available at any market. Hungarian salami knows no distribution shortfall (the

Budapest's Szazéves, for traditional style

Taste the quality at the Gerbeaud coffee-house

one everyone wants is called *téli szalami* or winter salami); there is spicy *csabai* and *gyulai* sausage, the gentle Trappist cheese (*trapista sajt*), and smoked *paranica* cheese.

Hungarians, being extremely hospitable, will readily invite you to their homes, where eating is a form of social intercourse. How many times have I heard the exhortation '*egyél, egyél*', eat, eat, when I could no longer even lift a fork!

Coffee-houses

The coffee-house is still a major institution in Hungary; Budapest in particular has a large number of them, of which the Gerbeaud, with its sumptous interior and pastries, is the most famous. The coffee-houses' creamy cakes, *tortes*, their fruit pies and *petits fours* will be a personal disaster for those visitors who visibly carry their calories around the waist. Try the *dobos torta*, layers of sponge cake and chocolate cream, the chocolate mousse concoction called *Rigó Jáncsi*, or the egregiously delicious *Somloi galuska*, a sponge base with nuts and chocolate and whipped cream.

A word on coffee is necessary, for tea, coming in bags, is not a speciality. The Turks brought coffee to Hungary, and the Magyars disliked it intensely at first, calling it black soup. That has changed. The coffee-houses offer the entire range, from *café au lait* to the light *mélange* (with cold milk or cream), to *cappuccino* and *espresso*. For a truly Hungarian experience, however, you must penetrate one of those neon-lit *pressző*, the equivalent of the French café, and drink an *eszpressző*. It may cure you of coffee permanently or make you a life-long addict.

And finally, on the subject of coffee: hotel breakfasts, even in the four- and five-star establishments, come with a thick black soup tasting strongly of chicory and healing muds. If you are a true caffeine addict, do not expect this to serve as a substitute. Real coffee is available, but you will be billed for it.

Look out for the locals

Budapest

BOHEMTANYA, Paulay Ede u. 16, off Deák tér. Tel: 122 1453. This is a popular and cheap place, always full, lively and genuine. The TÜKÖRY SÖRÖZŐ, Hold u. 15, Tel: 131 1931, is another of those popular places where the food is excellent and the ambience similar. The APROD, at Szondy u. 6, is a family-run business. If you are there at lunchtime, ask for the speciality of the day. SZARVAS ET-TEREM, on Szarvás tér 1 (at the foot of the castle), is more expensive and specialises in venison. The SZAZÉVES (Tel: 118 3608) and the MATYAS PINCE (Tel: 118 1650), both off Váci u., have good food, although the ye-olde-Budapest feeling is a bit contrived at times. Finally, for the more luxurious experience, there's the GUN-DEL, Allatkerti u. 2, Tel: 121 3550.

Szombathely

The HALASZCSARDA, the GYÖNGYÖS ETTEREM (Tel: 12-665) and the SAVARIA (Tel: 11-440) are most recommendable (see itineraries). The restaurant in the HOTEL CLAUDIUS, Bartók Béla körút 39, Tel: 13-760, is pleasant, light, clean and the food is good. Should you happen to be there after 11 November, make sure you try one of the goose specialities. Also attractive for its homeliness is MAG-YAR TENGER, Huszár u. 169 (direction Kőszeg), Tel: 11-644.

Pécs

The art-nouveau HOTEL PALATINUS (Rákóczi u. 3, Tel: 13-322) has a Söröző or beer hall with simple and good food. A little out of the way in town are the VADASZTANYA (Urögi u.), where you can find venison as a speciality, and various exotic dishes such as kangaroo; and the TETTYE ETTEREM, Tettye tér 4, which has Swabian specialities. The KALAMARIS (Rákóczi út 30, Tel: 12-573) has good Hungarian food, but makes attempts at something more modern.

Szeged

The HAGI, Kelemen u. 3, is a must, with fish a speciality. HALASZCSARDA FEHÉRTO, Külterület 41, also specialises in fish. ALABARDOS (Oskola u. 13, Tel: 12-914) is on the expensive side but the quality is high as well.

Debrecen

The restaurant of the ARANY BIKA on Piac u., Tel: 16-777, has a fair reputation. Neighbouring SZABADSAG is known for its lively crowds, but the food is solid home-cooking. For the FLASKA, Miklós u. 4, Tel: 14-582, you will need reservations. This tiny excellent restaurant specialises in hocks. About 12km (8 miles) on the way out to Hajdüszoboszló, the NADASCSARDA is open 24 hours day and quite recommendable, though it becomes a little raucous at night.

There are old-fashioned *csárdas* at regular intervals on the way out to Hortóbagy. They are all good and the ambience remains Hungarian in spite of the overwhelmingly foreign crowd in summer.

Eger

The FELLNER SÖRÖZŐ on Fellner J u. 3 in the centre of town (Tel: 10-417) is a popular place. The food is hearty, the service at times cranky. I'd recommend the TALIZMAN ETTEREM on Kossuth L. u. 25, near the entrance to the fort. Also in Eger are two restaurants, TULIPANKERT and KÖD-MÖN CSARDA, in the Szépasszony völgy, the Vale of the Pretty Woman, where many wine-makers have their cliff cellars. Atmospheric places – just watch out for the powerful Eger Bull's Blood wine. I suggest you avoid the restaurant under the cathedral.

Calendar of Special Events

If you see a gathering of Hungarians it is either a revolution festering or a festival in the making. The year in Hungary has its recurring feast days, of course – some are of religious or heathen origin, others political. The latter tend to celebrate lost causes (the revolutions of 1848 and of 1956), which might be unique in a world so in need of back-patting emblems of victory.

If you happen to be in Hungary for the Mardi Gras, drive down to Mohács on the Sunday before Ash Wednesday to participate in the *busójárás*, when young men dress in furs, put on huge wooden masks, and proceed to chase away the winter or evil spirits. At one time the *búsó* are said to have frightened off the Turks. Debrecen also has a noteworthy Mardi Gras parade.

Tourist offices can generally supply you with information on events. TOURINFORM, Sütő u. 2, 1052 Budapest, publishes a little booklet with the basics. It should be carried by your local Hungarian travel agent IBUSZ. The monthly *Programme* in Hungarian, German and English can be found *in situ* in tourist offices and hotels.

The Debrecen Flower Festival in full swing

MARCH

Hungary's first political celebration comes on 15 March, the day revolution broke out in 1848. Statues of the heroes of the day are covered with wreaths and Hungarian flags. It is a time for speeches.

The Spring Festival, during the second half of March, centres on Budapest. Hundreds of concerts, classical, jazz and folk, take place throughout the capital in concert halls and churches, and in several other towns (Sopron, Esztergom, Szentendre, Kecskemét, for example).

Painting Easter eggs in Hungary is an art of its own. Easter is celebrated in the time-honoured way, with processions on Good Friday, the blessing of hams and eggs on Sunday.

APRIL/MAY

May Day is traditionally marked by young men who decorate a branch with ribbons and offer it to a special girl. Whitsun also has its customs, and the coming of the warm season also means busy markets in many places, notably in Kalocsa.

JUNE/JULY/AUGUST

Horse shows are popular around this time (in Bugác, Szantódpuszta in mid-July, and Hortóbagy in August, for example). Performances frequently take place next to the Mátyás Church or on Disz tér in the Castle District of Budapest. The traditional opening of the Balaton season takes place in Balatonfüred with dances on 26 June. In July there's an opera festival on Cathedral Square in Szeged. Debrecen has its jazz days around then. Nyírbátor's music festival is in August.

On 20 August, the politico-religious feast of St István remembers the death of Hungary's first king and founder of the Hungarian state. Budapest has fireworks displays, and the Castle District is crammed with the stands of craftspeople. The biggest party, though, takes place in Calvinist Debrecen. The little town of Hortobágy bustles with the Hídivásár (19 and 20 August), a market held near the nine-arched bridge, and also on 20 August is the international Flower Festival of Debrecen. Games, Hungarian folklore, international folk performances and fireworks at night keep the celebrations going.

SEPTEMBER/OCTOBER

The wine regions (Balaton, Pécs, Eger, Tokaj, Kiskunság) have grape harvest celebrations. Budapest also hosts an arts festival in late September, which is nothing like the corresponding spring event. On 23 October the revolution of 1956 is commemorated, with speeches, demonstrations and heaps of wreaths on the proliferating memorials.

NOVEMBER/DECEMBER

November begins with All Saints' Day. Graves are made spick and span, cemeteries are lit with candles. St Martin's Day, 11 November, is celebrated with a traditional meal of goose, after which everyone sleeps.

Christmas and New Year are marked as they are in the West, with perhaps more sociability. Poppy seeds, a symbol of fertility, are baked into a kind of strudel (*makos beigli*) or eaten in a noodle dish called *makos guba*. Interestingly, Advent is not celebrated as it is in German-speaking countries, but with a wreath and four candles, a new one being lit each week. Children sometimes dress up and perform nativity plays.

PRACTICAL information

GETTING THERE

By Plane

Many airlines fly to Budapest's Ferihegy airport. MALÉV, Hungary's national airline, uses the Ferihegy II terminal, while all others use Ferihegy I. MALÉV is recommendable, particularly now that Italian airline Alitalia has become a 35 percent shareholder in the airline. New routes are being planned, and new planes bought (767s for long-distance flights). There are regular flights to and from all European capitals and major cities, several Balkan cities, a number of Middle Eastern cities (Damascus, Tel Aviv and Cairo, for example) and to New York.

MALÉV maintains a number of offices worldwide. **Canada**: Toronto, Tel: (416) 944-0093. **Israel**: Tel: (3) 524 6171. **UK**: London, Tel: (71) 439-0577 **US**: New York, Tel: (212) 757-6480, toll-free: (0800) 223 6884; Chicago, Tel: (312) 819 5353; Los Angeles, Tel: (310) 286 7980. In Hungary, most travel agents are in touch with the airline. MALÉV also has desks in the main Budapest hotels. Most international airlines flying to Hungary have offices in Budapest.

The regular and inexpensive bus service linking the airport with Deák tér in Pest is not currently available. Present options include a shared minibus, which should drop you at your hotel or wherever you

MALÉV is the national airline

want. For the return trip you can order the minibus to pick you up at a given location by telephoning 157 8993. A taxi from the airport should cost around three times as much as the minibus. Make sure the meter is running.

A final possibility is renting a car directly at the airport. Hertz and Avis, for example, have desks. For good value, however, you will have to shop around. And do not forget to ask if prices include the value added tax (VAT) which is currently at a stratospheric 25 percent. (*See Renting a Car below.*)

By Car

If you are starting in Budapest, you will probably want to drive in through Vienna, from which a motorway (A4) leads almost to the border crossing at Hegyeshalom. Listen to the radio in summer, as the queues here can be quite substantial. As an alternative you can try the Klingenbach/Sopron crossing about 70km

(44 miles) to the south of Vienna. At any rate there are more crossings further to the south. If driving through Carinthia in Austria, you may want to cut through Maribor, Slovenia (drivers here are several degrees worse than the Hungarians) and drive in through Letenye.

By Train

Trains from Western Europe, such as the Orient Express, usually arrive at the *Keleti pályaudvár*, the Eastern Station, in Budapest. If you happen to be a national requiring a visa, you will have to get it before boarding the train.

By Boat

A number of boats run by the Hungarian MAHART company and the Austrian DDSG-Donaureisen company operate hydrofoils and boats between Vienna and Budapest (and elsewhere). The trip is picturesque but not necessarily cheap. The boats land at Belgrád rakpart between Erzsébet and Szabadság bridges. Your local travel agent should be able to help you with information. You can also write to or call: DDSG-Donaureisen, Handelskai 265, A-1021 Wien, Tel: (0222) 217 500. Or try MAHART, Belgrád rakpart, Budapest V, Tel: 118 1704.

TRAVEL ESSENTIALS

When to Visit

Hungary is best from late March to October. Museums are open at this time, and numerous festivals take place (except the great Spring Festival which happens in the second half of March). The country blooms in various colours from May onward, first the fruit trees, then the sunflowers. Summer is often very hot (bring a bathing suit), but evenings can become quite chilly. September is a time of harvest especially in the wine-growing areas; there is also a small festival of performing arts in Budapest. The weather in October can be wonderful in lucky years, with the trees turning brilliant colours in the mountains. But it is cold. You can safely avoid the country in winter, unless you happen to be nearby: just about everything is closed.

Soaking up the sun

Customs

You must not import drugs or firearms (unless you are a hunter, and then you need a special permit from the consulate in your home country). CB transmitters and car telephones have to be registered at the border. If you are 16 or older, you are allowed 250 cigarettes, or 50 cigars, or 250 grams of tobacco, two litres of wine or one litre of spirits. The exporting of food is limited, but no one seems to really check unless you are doing it by the lorry-load. However, my wallet has been checked for currency on leaving the country: you are not allowed to take out more than 500 Forint, though there is a degree of tolerance here.

Passports

Europeans (except from Portugal, Greece and Turkey), Americans, members of the CIS, Canadians and Argentinians no longer need to buy the $25 visa before entering Hungary. Most Asians, Middle Easterners and Latin Americans do. Australians, New Zealanders and Maltese must have a visa. Apply at the consulate near you or, if driving or flying, pick one up at the border. However, this rule might have changed by the time this book goes to print!

Weather

Hungary's weather is still under Atlantic influence. It is warm to hot in summer with occasionally cool nights. Spring and autumn are moderate, with considerable amounts of rain.

Government and Economy

Hungary is a republic with a parliamentary democracy. Of the various political parties, the Hungarian Democratic Forum (MDF) is the strongest followed by the Free Democrats (SZDSZ), the Socialists and the Young Democrats (FDP). The economy is free-market, with a push to privatise the industries nationalised under the Communist government. The flag is red, white and green (*piros fehér zöld* in Hungarian) in horizontal bars. You will find these colours all over the place. Hungary has applied to become a member of the EC. It is a member of the World Monetary Fund and of the World Bank.

Geography

Hungary has a surface area of 93,036 sq km (36,000 sq miles) and a population of 10.5 million (1990). It is divided up into 19 counties (*megye*) that were originally created by King István I. Budapest, the capital, has 2 million inhabitants, the next largest city, Miskolc, 240,000. The economy is mainly agricultural, with husbandry (pork, chicken) and grain dominating. Industry is growing, but there is little ore (iron, bauxite, manganese). Tourism accounts for nearly 10 percent of the economy. The two largest rivers are the Tisza, with a 595km (370-mile) long section in the country, and the Danube, with 417km (260 miles). The highest point is the Kékestető in the Mátra mountains, at 1,015m (3,330ft). The lowest point is 78m (256ft) near Tiszasziget south of Szeged.

A gypsy girl

People

Hungarians like to point out that 30 percent of their nationals live abroad. Over 2 million in Romania, 750,000 in the US, 600,000 in Slovakia, 650,000 in ex-Yugoslavia, 220,000 in Israel, 200,000 in Ukraine, 140,000 in Canada, etc… They are talented people: among the internationally famous (or infamous) Hungarians you'll find Zsa-zsa Gabor, Tony Curtis, Peter Lorre, Ilona Staller (known as La Cicciolina, the porn star), Victor Vasarely, Franz Liszt, Béla Bartók, Zoltán Kodaly, Sir George Solti, György Czifra (concert halls are full of performing Hungarians), and Theodore Herzl, the founder of Zionism. When the British describe a ballpoint pen, they still use the name of its Hungarian inventor, Bíro. A chemist named János Irinyi discovered the striking match. And after the Gulf War, cheap and efficient Mig reactors were used to blow out the oil-well fires in Kuwait.

Currency

The Hungarian currency is the Forint, or the HUF for Eurocheque purposes. It divides up into 100 Fillér. The Forint comes in 5,000, 1,000, 500, 100 and 50 bills, rare are 20 and 10 Forint bills. There are also 20, 10, 5, 2 and 1 Forint coins. The Fillér comes in lightweight aluminium coins of 50, 20 and 10.

Hungary is currently cheaper than Western countries, but inflation is high, ranging between 25 and 35 percent.

The Forint is not a convertible currency, therefore exchanging it back into a hard currency will be costly. Only change as much as you need. The other symptom of inconvertibility is the fairly frequent occurrence of money-changers who offer better exchange rates on the street. These transactions are illegal. Furthermore, the money-changers are often shady fellows, who work in gangs and if you are tricked by them, you will have no legal recourse.

Eurocheques can be cashed in banks and most post offices. The acceptance of credit cards is also spreading rapidly, although it has not reached all petrol stations as yet.

Should you not be using a car, then Hungary has trains and buses to offer. Both can be a little uncomfortable at times as the vehicles are not always state-of-the-art. The national railway MÁV has offices in most towns, but for schedules and reservations any Hungarian travel agent should do. MÁV's central number in Budapest is 142-9150. The Volán bus company also has a central number: 118 7315. Warning: the Matészalka-Budapest train is notoriously rowdy on Friday evenings from and on Sunday evenings to the capital. Avoid it!

Trams still run in Budapest

By Air

Air Service operates small planes between Hungarian towns. The central number in Budapest is 138 4867. It also provides charter planes, hot-air balloons, air excursions, air photos, crop dusting, etc. Prices are moderate, as the following sample prices show: Budapest to Debrecen 2,770 Forint, Szombathely to Nyíregyháza 4,620 Forint, Győr to Szeged 3,630 Forint.

Renting a Car

Shopping around for car hire is always best, as prices vary drastically. Off-season is cheaper (from October to April), and renting locally in Hungary itself is usually cheaper, though not necessarily less complicated.

Make sure, when prices are quoted, that everything is included and then, when you pick up the vehicle, that it is properly tanked up. There are rental agencies at the airport as well.

Főtaxi-Hertz, Tel: 122 1471
Ibusz-Avis, Tel: 118 4240, at Ferihegy

airport terminal I: 147 5754, terminal II: 157 8470.

Volántourist-Europcar, Tel: 133 4783, at Ferihegy airport terminal I: 134 2540, terminal II: 157 8570.

Driving

If you are driving in Hungary you should be aware of several facts:

1) The driver is not allowed to drink *at all.* Violations are dealt with severely.

2) Stick to the speed limits: 120kph (75mph) on the motorways, 100kph (62mph) on main highways, 80kph (50mph) on lesser roads, 60kph (37mph) in villages, unless otherwise indicated.

3) Be careful, especially at night. Hungarians tend to ride bicycles, horse-driven carts and other vehicles without lights.

3) Hungarians are, with all due respect, by and large criminally poor drivers (no doubt offenders think quite differently about themselves). They tailgate, overtake on blind bends, honk if you are not exceeding the speed limit as they are, and race through crowded villages. In short, they break every written and unwritten law in the book and are proud of it. The number of dead animals by the side of the road and the high accident rate testify to their skills. The availability of Western cars has only made matters worse. This style is often imitated by foreigners, unfortunately.

4) Road quality varies. Small roads are generally in poor shape, and the farther east you drive the worse they get. The highways are well surfaced.

5) The refuelling network even for unleaded fuel has grown in leaps and bounds in the past few years. Many stations (though not the state-run Áfor) stay open 24 hours. Generally there is no self-service, though it is sometimes expedient to overlook this custom. A small tip is encouraged, especially if the pumper also cleans the windows. Cost of petrol is about the same as in the rest of Europe. Diesel is cheaper.

I suggest you do not drive in Budapest. Parking is difficult, traffic is thick and fast. Make sure your car is empty, and remove the radio if possible. Robbery is comparatively frequent.

A hazard for motorists

In case of accident: no matter how minor, call the police (07). The ambulance number is 04.

Repairs: if you come with your own car make sure it is in good condition before the trip. Repairs may not be available locally. Towing insurance is advisable. The Hungarian automobile club (*Magyar Autoclub*) is fairly efficient: Budapest, Tel: 252 2800. The network of emergency phones on the motorways is growing.

Motorcyclists must wear helmets and keep their headlights on during the day.

Driver's glossary

Autopálya = motorway
Bejárat/kijárat = ramp/exit
Híd = bridge
Rév = ferry
Tér = square
Útépítés = road repairs
Út (sometimes utja) = road, avenue
Utca (abbr. u.) = street
Vasút = railway
Vigyazz! = Beware!

Maps

Maps are available in Hungary at a good price. A good choice is the *Magyarország Autóatlasza*, the Road Atlas of Hungary, with maps, a list of hotels (with explanation in English, German, French and Russian to boot) and a section with small maps of towns, cities and villages listing their sights in basic Hungarian.

HOURS AND HOLIDAYS

Business Hours

Most services keep operating somewhere within the normal business day, ie, from 9am–5pm weekdays and 9am–noon on Saturdays. Banks close usually by 4.30pm

and stay closed on Saturday, but hotels and tourist bureaux will change money for you and post offices will take Eurocheques. Shops tend to close about midday (between 12.30 and 2pm), but not supermarkets. Evening closing hours begin at 6pm for department stores, and go on until 8pm for supermarkets. This rule is not universally applied, however. On Thursdays shops often stay open longer.

A symptom of capitalist fever, and one that makes life very convenient for consumers, is the proliferation of 24-hour shops, which sometimes charge a little more at night.

Public Holidays

1 January, New Year
15 March , beginning of the Revolution of 1848, gatherings at the statues of Petőfi, Kossuth, Bem and other anti-Habsburg moguls.
Easter Monday
20 August, death of István I, founder of the Hungarian state. Fireworks, festivals (Bridge Market in Hortobágy, Flower Festival in Debrecen, crafts market in Budapest's Castle District).
23 October, beginning of the 1956 rebellion against Stalin and Stalinism. It started at the Bem statue in Buda, and that is where people gather. Very emotional. Many of the old leaders give speeches.
Christmas Day and Boxing Day

ACCOMMODATION

Not all of Hungary is as prepared for a gigantic onslaught of tourists as are the Balaton region and Budapest. If you are planning a trip in August, beware of Formula One racing time at the Hungaroring. It fills up Budapest's hotel rooms. A few things you should know about overnight stays: first, many of the modern hotels built in the 1960s and 1970s are not well soundproofed, and the furnishings leave something to be desired (carpets are worn, beds are short and soft). The prices are frequently too high for the value. The one consistent problem I have found, however, is noise, be it from poorly-placed ventilation shafts or chugging water pipes, or from cleaning crews merrily chattering away at 6am just outside the door of my room. There are, of course, good hotels available at very reasonable rates.

HungarHotels is an international chain, with a reservation office in Budapest at Petőfi Sándor u. 16, Tel: 118-3393. Your local IBUSZ office will also be able to make reservations for you.

A fairly inexpensive way to go is to rent private rooms through IBUSZ or another Hungarian travel agent. The cost is from 400 Forint upward, and this method gives you a little insight into how people in Hungary live. (The sofa may not always be very comfortable.) And then there is bed-and-breakfast accommodation (*panzió*), though those with more modern facilities match hotel prices. Hungary has good camping sites.

Hotels

The following is a small selection of hotels in the cities used as centres in this book. Price categories are as follows: $$$ = US$120 and up; $$ = US$60–119; $ = US$15–59. Note that hotels in Budapest and Balaton are likely to be up to 20 percent more expensive than elsewhere.

Budapest

International chains have their luxury hotels in the city: Atrium Hyatt, Intercontinental, Hilton and Béke (Radisson), for example. You get all services here. The Balloon Room of the Atrium-Hyatt is a bar with a reputation for its very pretty and expensive women (all $$$). More moderately priced and pleasant are:

THE ASTORIA
Kossuth L u. 19, Tel: 117-3411
This old-fashioned hotel is not quiet but it has atmosphere. *$$*

THE TAVERNA
Váci u. 20, Tel: 139-4999
In the middle of the action. It is nevertheless quiet, clean, very agreeable. *$$*

THE CITADELLA
Citadella sétány, Tel: 166-5794
It overlooks Budapest, is small, comfortable and cheap. *$*

Szombathely

CLAUDIUS
Bartók Béla krt. 39, Tel: 94/13-760
1970s vintage, cement, rooms are on the shoddy side for the prices. *$$*

SAVARIA
Mártirok tere, Tel: 94/11-440
A charming place, whose rooms are not as pretty as the hotel's art nouveau facade might lead you to expect. *$*

LIGET
Szt. István park 4, Tel: 94/14-168
Offers the basics. *$*

Pécs

HUNYOR
Jurisics M u 16, Tel: 72/15-677
A large, modern hotel with all the amenities and unfortunately cement floors, which tend to transfer sound terribly well. *$$*

MEDITERRAN
Dömörkapu: very pleasant location up in the hills above Pécs, Tel: 72/15987
Don't take the small suite on the top floor: a ventilator from the heating room grinds all night over the window. A brilliant architect was at work. *$$*

PALATINUS
Kossuth L u. 5, Tel: 72/33-022
This beautiful art nouveau building is an experience. *$$*

Rural idyll

Szeged

HUNGARIA
Komócsin Z tér 2, Tel: 62/21-211
For details see the Claudius in Szombathely. $$

NAPFÉNY
Dorozsmai út 4 (on the way to Route 5, Kecskemét) from the centre, Tel: 62/25-800
It's a kind of motel, no frills but affordable. $

TISZA
Wesselényi u. 1, Tel: 62/12-466
Upmarket, fine old place in the middle of town. $

Debrecen

ARANY BIKA
Piac u. 11-15, Tel: 52/16-777
An older and rather dignified hotel in the town centre. $$

CIVIS
Kálvin tér 4, Tel: 52/18-522. $

FŐNIX
Barna u. 17, Tel: 52/13-355. $

Debrecen
Petőfi tér 9, Tel: 52/16-550
The last three are basic hotels with basic prices. $

Eger

EGER
Szálloda u. 1-3, Tel: 36/13-233
Big, mid-scale, modern, not cosy. $$

FLORA
Klapka u. 8, Tel: 36/ 13-233. $$

MINARET
Harangöntő u. 3-5, Tel: 36/20-233
This is a very affordable, pleasant place at a terrific location near the Minaret. $

UNICORNIS
Dr Hibay K. u. 2, Tel: 36/12-886
Basic hotel material, not too expensive. $

NIGHTLIFE

The capital is full of late-night bars, some of rather dubious nature. One of my favourites is the **Pierrot** up in the Castle District, because it has a real piano bar. There are discos, notably the Petfi Csarnók in the city park (*Városliget*), where, according to the aficionados, hellzapoppin, and revues that are not especially exciting.

The provinces are not as lively. A good general bet are the larger hotels. In Debrecen there are two nightspots of a certain size, the **Rozsakert**, which serves food quite late and where dancing is outside in summer, and the **Új Vigadó**, where the crowd is on the younger side. The bar **Arany Bika** is open late, as is the **Szabadság étterem** next door. The latter has good food but, according to friends there, after a certain point it does tend to get rather riotous.

Thanks to the university, Szeged does have some spots, though the one I landed in near the Napfény Hotel (Dorozsmai út 4) left me almost deaf. Asking the hotel reception for the newer places is a good idea. The same applies to Pécs (also a university town). Up in the Tettye quarter is a restaurant where a two-man band offers nice ballroom tunes. And on Széchenyi tér, next to the old Nádor Hotel is a little disco with dim lights, 1970s furniture and a small bar, where the ambience is acceptable.

Eger and Szombathely are even quieter. Under the cathedral of Eger is a labyrinthine restaurant and nightspot. Having eaten an awful meal there, I must confess to having taken to the hills before the fun started.

HEALTH AND EMERGENCIES

No vaccinations are needed before going to Hungary, but you should have normal travel insurance with all the benefits, for in an emergency, you may wish to avoid a stay in a Hungarian hospital. They are not up to Western standards yet. AIDS is a growing problem especially in Budapest, so do take precautions if enjoying a chance encounter. The food may be on the heavy side, but this can be counteracted by ample amounts of fresh fruit (remember to wash it) and vegetables available at local markets or by the side of the road. Hungarian supermarkets also carry health waters (*gyógyvíz*) that are mildly purgative. Be equipped for heavy sun in summer, and dip into as many lakes and pools as you can find on the way. Their suitability is indicated by a blue sign showing a stick figure swimming. Every now and then a little epidemic of something breaks out. Usually everyone knows about it. In the early 1990s, for example, there were several cases of dysentery reported from the River Tisza.

For small problems approach the local pharmacy (*gyógyszertár*). If you need a doctor (*orvos*) ask the pharmacy, the hotel reception or your host. For emergencies dial 04.

A word about toilets is necessary at this point: always bring your own toilet roll with you, even if you are in a 'good' establishment. And keep change handy for the attendant.

Spas

Hungary has innumerable spa facilities from 16th-century Turkish baths to highly modern places like the Hotel Termal on Margit Island in Budapest. Some of the spas are natural wonders, such as the cavern baths of Miskolctapolca or the warmwater lake of Hévíz. The waters of Hungary are indicated against a variety of disorders from arthritis to tracheitis. If you are prone to circulatory illness or

Necessary facility

suffer from allergies, ask your physician what you should avoid, as not all waters are good for you. The Hungarian Tourist Board publishes several brochures on the subject of spas available at IBUSZ offices.

Letters please

Crime

Crime is steeply on the rise in Hungary, particularly in Budapest. Most common is larceny, breaking into cars, picking pockets and the like. Do take the usual precautions.

COMMUNICATIONS

Post

Post offices are open Monday to Friday 8am–6pm except in smaller towns and villages, and from 8am–2pm at the latest on Saturdays. The post offices at the western and eastern train stations in Budapest are open all night and Sundays.

Telephone

Telephones in Hungary were excellent before World War II, according to the older generation. The generation of public phones left over from the communist years is frustrating (they are yellow and red, and take 5, 10 and 20 Forint coins). If they work, they will be most probably on a loud thoroughfare, making conversation difficult. A new generation of card telephones is emerging, but I must withhold comment as to their robustness. At least they will not be ripped out of the booths by gangs of felons, a common fate for the previous phones.

Telephoning in hotels is quite expensive. Some parts of the country are being restructured and the telephone numbers are being changed. If you are having trouble reaching a place (say for reservations or urgency), send a telegram.

Dialling long-distance in Hungary: 06 – wait for the tone – dial prefix and number.

Information in foreign languages: dial 117 2200.

Dialling internationally: dail the international access code 00, then the relevant country code: Australia (61); Canada (1); Germany (49); Italy (39); Japan (81); the Netherlands (31); Spain (34); United Kingdom (44); United States (1). If you

Learning Hungarian is not easy

are using a US phone credit card dial the company's access number as follows: AT&T, Tel: 00* 800-01111; MCI, Tel: 00* 800-01411; Sprint, Tel: 00* 800-01877.

LANGUAGE

German and increasingly English are spoken by Hungarians, especially in the touristically trodden areas, including Budapest, Lake Balaton, Pécs, and Szeged. Where this is not the case try sign language and drawing. The problem is that Hungarian words often have no resemblance whatsoever to Indo-European words. *Rendőrség* means police, a *vendéglő* is a restaurant, *szálloda* means hotel

(though the word hotel is used too). You are dealing with a Finno-Ugric language whose roots go back to the 7th millennium BC and to the Urals. It is, however, sheer myth that the Hungarians and Finns understand each other. Barring a handful of ancient words recalling a common past (such as *vaj* for butter), only linguists can explain the link.

Learning Hungarian can be fun. Use of aspirin is recommended. Beware of pronunciations:

a	=	a as in car
á	=	open a as in after
c	=	ts
e	=	e as in especially
é	=	a as in bare (distinction of e and the long é is very important: *segg* means backside, and *ség*, see the toast below, is a common suffix: eg. *hidegség* means cold, *hidegseg* means cold backside).
gy	=	a run together
i	=	short ee
í	=	long ee
ly	=	long i with a sound, a kind of yuh
ny	=	nyuh
ty	=	a slightly aspirated tyuh (tyuk = tee-ook)
o	=	short o as in horror
ó	=	long o as in Poland
ö	=	e as in perfect
ő	=	same as ö but longer
s	=	sh
sz	=	s
u	=	oo
ú	=	oooo
ü	=	same as in German, or u in French
ű	=	same as ü but longer
zs	=	who does not know Zsa-zsa Gabor?

Emphasis is always on the first syllable. The language is agglutinative, which means two things. First you stick prepositions, personal articles, and a variety of case suffixes at the end of the word. The result is, for example, "Healthyourto!" (*Egészségünkre!*). Like the Germans, Hungarians also stick words together: *fagylaltkülönlegességek* means ice-cream specialities. Verbs, on the other hand, come apart but not with Germanic regularity. Among the strangest floating particles is the famous *meg*, which indicates a completed action. Secondly, it means that there is little room for a pig-Hungarian, since the juxtaposition of undeclined verbs and nouns gives no meaning.

There are dozens of case suffixes and most come in two versions, one soft (to be vocally harmonised with the letters a, o, u; and one sharp (for the other letters). For example: *szobában* (in the room), *vendéglőben* (in the restaurant). Some suffixes assimilate with the last letter of the noun: *autóval* (by car), *vonattal* (from *vonatval*, by train).

The Akadémiai Kiadó publishes a nice little Hungarian-English dictionary that you can find in most larger bookstores in Hungary. Cost is minimal, and it will help you plough through menus, headlines and some museum titles.

Proper names

Jenő = Eugene *Molnár* = Miller
Antal = Anthony *Kertész* = Gardener
Imre = Emmerich *Varga* = Cobbler
István = Steven *Király* = King
Mihály = Michael *Asztalos* = Carpenter
János = John *Kádár* = Cooper
Győző = Victor *Kovács* = Smith
Margit = Margaret *Bodor* = Curly

Common words and phrases

Numbers = *Egy, kettő, három, négy, öt, hat, hét, nyolc, kilenc, tíz. Tizenegy, tizenkettő,... Húsz* (20), *harminc, negyven, ötven, hatvan, hétven, nyolcvan, kilencven, szász* (100). *Ezer* (1000).
Days: Monday to Sunday: *hétfő, kedd, szerda, csütörtök, péntek, szombat, vásárnap.*
Igen, nem = yes, no
Bocsánat = pardon (for stepping on your toe, eg)
Elnézést = excuse me, (what time is it? eg)
Jó reggelt kívánok = Good morning!
Jó napot kívánok = Good day!
Jó estét kívánok = Good evening!
Jó éjszakát kívánok = Good night!
Jó étvágyat kívánok = Bon appétit!
Viszontlátásra = Goodbye! (often colloquially *visz'lát*)
Please = *kérem szépen*
Thank you = *köszönöm szépen*
How much is it? = *Mennyibe kerül?*
Is there ...? = *Van ... ?*

I'd like to pay = *fizetni (kérem)*
Where is ...? = *Hol...?*
left/right/straight = *balra/jobbra/egyenesen*
Naturally = *persze*
Hotel = *hotel, szálloda*
Double/single room = *kétágyás/egyágyás szoba*
Bathroom = *Fürdőszoba*
Toilet = *WC, toalett, mosdó*
Ladies/gents = *női, férfi*
Shop = *bolt, üzlet*
Price = *ár*
Closed/open = *zárva/nyítva*
Help = *segítség!*
Leave me alone = *Hagyj békén* (fairly polite)
Doctor = *orvos*
Ambulance = *Mentőauto*
Police = *rendőrség*

Finally, a frequently heard word is *tessék*. It is universally applied and can mean please (inviting you to help yourself); it is the way to answer a telephone, a waiter will approach you with the words *tessék parancsolni* (please, order); it can also mean 'there you go' as in proving a point.

Riding is one of the national sports, and it is practised throughout the country, especially, however on the Great Plain. Swimming, too, is a Hungarian speciality. Lake Balaton is only one example: Try Lake Velence west of Budapest or the Kiskőre reservoir south of Tiszafüred (Abádszalok is the name of the resort). Every town has at least one large swimming-pool and many have spas. Lake

Fun park on Lake Balaton

Finding your own way is not hard

Balaton is also a sailing paradise, but watch out for violent storms: a yellow rocket means a storm is on its way, and a red rocket means head for shore.

Tennis is also on the rise, with many hotels building courts for their clients and increasing numbers of clubs. For all questions, the best place to turn to is TOURINFORM, Sütő u. 2, Budapest. Anglers and hunters wanting a permit and needing the latest rules should write to MAVAD, Úri u. 39, Budapest.

Hungary also has some skiing mainly around the Kékestető in the Mátra mountains. There is also a ski jump here, but of course one has to have a white winter.

MUSEUMS

You will find ample museums beyond those mentioned in this book. A sign showing a sketchy neoclassical building on a blue background indicates something worth seeing. Often the word *múzeum* is written under it. When you see a sign saying *tájház* it means a regional house turned into a museum. Not all museums are equipped for foreigners, especially those out in the far reaches. Most are usually open from 10am to 6pm and are generally closed on Monday.

In Budapest, the museums are not so well signposted. If you have an extra day or two, visit the museums of the Castle (Buda), with its historic exhibitions. In Pest do not miss the Museum of Applied Arts (Iparművészeti Múzeum) on Üllői út, housed in a beautiful art nouveau building by Ödön Lechner. There are also tours of the Parliament, and opposite, on Kossuth tér, is the Ethnographic Museum. On the way to Szentendre you

will pass the Roman settlement of *Aquincum*, which also has a museum.

USEFUL ADDRESSES

Tourist Offices

IBUSZ is Hungary's long-standing travel agent, and has been privatised. It has offices in many parts of the world:

Chicago: IBUSZ, 233 North Michigan Ave, Suite 1308, Chicago Illinois, 60601, Tel: (312)819-3150. London: Danube Travel, Ltd, 6 Conduit Street, London W1R 9TG, Tel: (71) 493-0263. New York: IBUSZ, One Parker Plaza, Suite 1104, Fort Lee, New Jersey 07024, Tel: (201)592-8585.

Tourist offices are also omnipresent, beginning with border crossings, the airport, and train stations. They provide numerous services including hotel reservations, changing money, etc.

If you are staying in a more expensive hotel, you will probably have a tourist office located somewhere in the lobby. A vital number is the international Tourist Information Service TOURINFORM in Budapest, Sütő u. 2, Tel: 117 9800. Alternatives are:

Budapest Tourist, Roosevelt tér 5, Tel: 117 3555

Cooptourist, Kossuth L tér 13-15, Tel: 112 1017

Hungarotours, Akácfa u. 20, Tel: 141 3889

IBUSZ Hotel Service, Petőfi tér 3, Tel: 118 5707

Debrecen: Hajdú Tourist, Kálvin tér 2A, Tel: (52) 10820

Advertising the arts

Riverscape near Szeged

Eger: Eger Tourist: Bajcsy-Zilinsky u. 9, Tel: (36) 13249

Kecskémet: Pusztatourist, Szabadság tér 2, Tel: (76) 29499

Keszthely: IBUSZ, Széchenyi u. 1-3, Tel (82) 12951

Miskolc: Borsod Tourist, Széchenyi u. 35, Tel: (46) 35946

Nyíregyháza: Nyírtourist, Dózsa Gy. u. 3, Tel: (42) 11544

Pécs: Mecsek Tourist, Széchenyi tér 9, Tel: (72) 13300

Szeged: Szeged Tourist, V. Hugo u. 1, Tel: (62) 11711.

Sopron: Ciklamén Tourist, gabona tér 8, Tel: (99) 12040

Székesfehérvár Albatours, Szabadság tér 6, Tel: (22) 12818

Szombathely: Savaria Tourist, Martírok tere 1, Tel (94) 12348

Foreign Embassies in Budapest

Austria
VI, Benczúr utca 16. Tel: 121 3213

Germany
XIV, Stefánia út 101–103. Tel: 251 8999
Consulate: Nógrádi utca 8, Tel: 155 9366

Switzerland
XIV, Stefánia út 107. Tel: 122 9491

United Kingdom
V, Harmincad utca 6. Tel: 118 2888

United States
V, Szabadság tér 12. Tel: 112 6450

FURTHER READING

Apa Publications, *Insight Guide: Hungary* (2nd edition 1991), a comprehensive guide to the history, culture and sights, beautifully illustrated.

Apa Publications, *Insight Pocket Guide: Budapest* (1993).

László Cseke, *The Danube Bend* (1977; originally published in Hungarian, 1976), explores the Danube landscape.

C A Macartney, *Hungary: A Short History* (1962).

Ferenc Molnár, *The Paul Street Boys* (1907). A classic work of Hungarian literature.

Gyula Németh (ed), *Hungary: A Complete Guide*, translation from the Hungarian, 3rd revised edition (1988), discusses the history and environs of Hungary.

Martyn C Rady, *Medieval Buda: A Study of Municipal Government and Jurisdiction in the Kingdom of Hungary* (1985), the most authoritative work on the subject.

T I Berend and G Ránki, *Hungary: A Century of Economic Development* (1974).

Emeric W Trencsényi (comp.), *British Travellers in Old Budapest* (1973), a collection of descriptions of the capital of Hungary.

Index

ACKNOWLEDGMENTS

Photography **Márton Radkai** *and*
Pages 35т & в, 83 **Katherine Radkai**
33т, 50, 87 **Hans-Horst Skupy**

Cover Design **Klaus Geisler**
Handwriting **V. Barl**
Cartography **Berndtson & Berndtson**

INSIGHT GUIDES

COLORSET NUMBERS

You'll find the colorset number on the spine of each Insight Guide.

INSIGHT *pocket* GUIDES

• •

United States: **Houghton Mifflin Company, Boston MA 02108
Tel: (800) 2253362 Fax: (800) 4589501**

Canada: **Thomas Allen & Son, 390 Steelcase Road East
Markham, Ontario L3R 1G2
Tel: (416) 4759126 Fax: (416) 4756747**

Great Britain: **GeoCenter UK, Hampshire RG22 4BJ
Tel: (256) 817987 Fax: (256) 817988**

Worldwide: **Höfer Communications Singapore 2262
Tel: (65) 8612755 Fax: (65) 8616438**

" I was first drawn to the Insight Guides by the excellent "Nepal" volume. I can think of no book which so effectively captures the essence of a country. Out of these pages leaped the Nepal I know – the captivating charm of a people and their culture. I've since discovered and enjoyed the entire Insight Guide Series. Each volume deals with a country or city in the same sensitive depth, which is nowhere more evident than in the superb photography. "

Sir Edmund Hillary

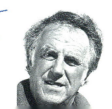